John Knox and the
Town Council of Edinburgh

John Knox and the
Town Council of Edinburgh

With a Chapter on
The So-called "John Knox's House"

By
Robert Miller
Lord Dean of Guild

WIPF & STOCK · Eugene, Oregon

Wipf and Stock Publishers
199 W 8th Ave, Suite 3
Eugene, OR 97401

John Knox and the Town Council of Edinburgh
With a Chapter on the So-called "John Knox's House"
By Miller, Robert
Softcover ISBN-13: 978-1-6667-8041-3
Hardcover ISBN-13: 978-1-6667-8042-0
eBook ISBN-13: 978-1-6667-8043-7
Publication date 5/16/2023
Previously published by Andrew Eliot, 1898

This edition is a scanned facsimile of the original edition
published in 1898.

Preface

THE following pages are the outcome of an investigation that I have made into the possibility of locating accurately any residence of Knox in Edinburgh. The third chapter may be regarded as the body of the work, which branched out later into the wider field from which I have taken the title. The first two Chapters are in this light introductory and explanatory, and the last chapter—that on the so-called "John Knox's House"—comes in as an Appendix to the conclusions arrived at in Chapter III. Readers of the book who are acquainted with the difficulties of antiquarian research will readily understand the enormous amount of time and labour that goes to produce a very few pages of original work, but I may be allowed to state here for the benefit of what is called the "ordinary reader" that no trace of the greatest and

Preface

heaviest part of the work involved will be found in the results. Whole bundles of papers were gone through time after time without finding anything germane to my purpose, and clues were pursued often for months, only to find at the end that the scent was false.

The inquiry into Mowbray's house was facilitated somewhat by the site of the building having been acquired recently by the Corporation of Edinburgh. It was very interesting to find—what had not been suspected and which it took me a considerable time to discover—that John Knox lived during the greater part of his career in Edinburgh on a site that is to be occupied in the immediate future by the Town Council of the Burgh. The quotations given from the Records show how intimate were the relations between Knox and the Council in the early years of this period. After having thus, with considerable difficulty, located Mowbray's house, I instituted a fresh examination of documents with a view to discovering if any indications could

Preface

be found that might guide to the site of the John Adamson's house referred to in the Council Records in 1568 and 1569. I regret that the result of this portion of the investigation is not so definite as I should like, but the examination of documents has shown for the first time the neighbourhood in which Adamson's house—whichever one of the three which he possessed it may have been—was situated.

I have to acknowledge in connection with this latter part of the work, valuable assistance given me by Mr J. A. Wenley, Treasurer of the Bank of Scotland, in granting access to various Inventories of Title-deeds belonging to the Bank, which was the owner of much of Adamson's former property. These Inventories, along with certain old plans, enabled me to trace more readily than would otherwise have been possible, the connection between the owners in 1568 and 1898, and rendered easier an exact identification of the sites concerned.

I now publish the conclusions arrived at as

Preface

being the result of a thoroughly independent investigation into the question of the residence of Knox in Edinburgh. My official connection with the Town Council of Edinburgh for several years back as Lord Dean of Guild gave me special facilities for such an enquiry. The only merit I claim is that of careful research. I had no particular view to defend or controvert, and, as a matter of fact, I had to change my opinions on many points many times, as fresh evidence came to light.

ROBERT MILLER.

38 Lauder Road,
Edinburgh, *October* 1898.

Contents

		PAGE
I.	SCOTLAND AND EDINBURGH BEFORE 1560	1
II.	PAYMENTS MADE BY THE TOWN COUNCIL FOR JOHN KNOX AND THE MINISTERS	23
III.	HOUSES OCCUPIED BY JOHN KNOX IN EDINBURGH	63
IV.	THE LEGEND OF "JOHN KNOX'S HOUSE"	113
	NOTES TO CHAPTER IV.	161
	INDEX	170

Scotland and Edinburgh
before 1560

Scotland and Edinburgh before 1560

THE nineteenth century has been for Scotland in the main a time of continued peace. Those who live in its closing years can hardly realise how novel a state of things this is north of the Tweed, and how quietness and Scotland were formerly anything but synonymous terms.

When Scott gave his first novel of "Waverley" the sub-title of "'Tis Sixty Years Since," he brought before our grandfathers a condition of society which was very far removed from anything that could by the greatest stretch of courtesy be called civilisation now. The Wizard of the North described life in "Waverley" as it had been in Scotland a hundred and fifty years ago. Even when he wrote, the life he pictured

John Knox & Edinburgh

had disappeared and was being forgotten. But far back, behind "Waverley," there was a tumultuous history of Edinburgh into which the great magician has also allowed us to glance. Before 1805, with its interest for us all, there had been 1745, with its life of romance and adventure, but before 1745 there had been a 1545; and the stirring times of 1745 were, as compared with it, only as water unto wine.

Edinburgh had been captured in 1544 by an English force under the Earl of Hertford. The city was set on fire, and burned for three days; and very few of the buildings, constructed as they nearly all were of clay, wood, and straw, can possibly have escaped. Smarting under a defeat at Ancrum Moor, the English returned again the following year, and completed a victorious march through the south of Scotland, by destroying all that the citizens of Edinburgh had built within the past few months. The whole border district of Scotland between the Forth and the Cheviots was laid waste in this raid of 1545,

Edinburgh before 1560

and it is to the visitors from England—"our auld enemies of England," as they are called in the Statute Book—that we owe the stately ruins of the Border Abbeys of Jedburgh, Kelso, Dryburgh, and Melrose. The work of destruction was rendered more complete if possible in Edinburgh during the English occupation of the city after the disastrous battle of Pinkie in 1547, when the Abbey Church of Holyrood was given over to the flames. Edinburgh has, mainly in consequence of these raids, no buildings older than the second half of the sixteenth century, with the exception of the church of St Giles and portions of the Castle, and the walls of the north-west tower of Holyrood and the ruined walls of its chapel.

The Scottish people turned in their distress to their old ally France, and the key to the troubled period that ensued is to be found in the question whether French or English influence was to be dominant in the politics of Scotland. The situation was complicated by the storm of the Reformation, which had

John Knox & Edinburgh

not yet reached Scotland as an active force, though its murmur was already felt. George Wishart was burned for heresy at St Andrews in 1545. In the next year, 1546, the Cardinal Archbishop of St Andrews was murdered in his own castle by a band of conspirators, no doubt largely in retaliation for Wishart's death. The castle was held afterwards by the archbishop's assassins for fourteen months in defiance of the Regent, until a French force was brought over in sixteen galleys, and an attack opened upon the rebels both by sea and land. The English army had retired southward after the final destruction of Edinburgh in 1547, but another invasion took place in the following year under the Earl of Surrey—invasions had now become almost annual—and an appeal was made to France for help. A French fleet landed at Leith on the 16th of June 1548, with an army of 6000 foreign auxiliaries and a supply of cannon, and the work of driving the English out of Scotland was nearly completed when peace was arranged in 1550. Meantime, the

Edinburgh before 1560

young Queen, so well-known afterwards as Mary Queen of Scots, had been sent to France for security. She remained there as maiden, wife, and widow for nearly thirteen years.

"For a few years now," to quote Hill Burton's History of Scotland, "the country was peaceful, and therefore for historical purposes nearly a blank. As a contemporary puts it, 'every man addressed himself to policy, and to plant, and plenish those places which through the troubles of the wars, by English or others, had been wasted, burnt, spoiled, or destroyed.'"[1] When war next broke out, it was between two parties within Scotland itself, and was carried on largely under the name of religion. A riot in Edinburgh in 1558, when an image of St Giles, the patron saint of the town, was ducked in the North Loch and afterwards burned, marks the outbreak of a civil strife which was protracted for over fourteen years. The war— for war it may be regarded to have been

[1] "History of Scotland," Edition 1897, Vol. III., p. 281.

John Knox & Edinburgh

during all this time — was originally one between the Crown on the one side and a body of the Scottish nobles, enrolled under the name of "Lords of the Congregation," on the other. The Crown had the support of France in the earlier stages of the war as the defender of the old-established state of affairs in religious matters; the Lords of the Congregation had the general support of Queen Elizabeth in the prosecution of their designs, since they professed to have taken arms in defence of those principles of the Reformation that had already become dominant in Geneva and England, and were also asserting themselves strongly in France. It was agreed early in the struggle that the French troops should go home; but the fortunes of Mary and the old religion seemed, nevertheless, on the point of triumphing, when all was lost by her ill-judged marriage with Bothwell, and the subsequent defeat at Langside in 1567, which was followed by the flight of Mary into England. In spite of this her cause was not yet despaired of, and

Edinburgh before 1560

Edinburgh Castle was still held for the Queen in 1572, when the news arrived of the massacre of the Huguenots in France on St Bartholomew's Day. This sealed the overthrow of the former regime in the Church, and the principles advocated by the party of reform were accepted by the Parliament of Scotland.

The popular hero of this struggle is John Knox. He was one of those who had been captured in the Castle of St Andrews after the murder of the Archbishop in 1546, and had acted as religious adviser to the conspirators. He served for nineteen months as a slave on the French galleys, and spent five years in England after his release, and five more on the Continent where he pursued that "call" to the ministry which he had received at St Andrews. He had in the meantime visited Scotland in 1555, and had been cited to appear before the Bishops to answer a charge of heresy. This resulted in his condemnation after he had retired to Geneva, and his being burnt in effigy at the Cross of Edinburgh.

John Knox & Edinburgh

He started again for Scotland in 1557, but was stopped at Dieppe; and he arrived finally in Edinburgh in 1559, when he judged the times to be ripe for his designs. The Bishops of the old Church seemed ready to allow judgment to go against them by default, and it was not through any exertions on the part of its rulers that the ultimate victory of the Reformation was postponed until 1572. A visit made by Knox to Perth immediately after his return to Scotland resulted in the sacking of the churches and monasteries of that city by the mob. He came back to Edinburgh by way of Dundee, and attempted to guide the fortunes of the Reformation from the capital until his death, with the exception of two periods when Edinburgh was not judged a safe place of residence for himself or his friends. He was thus absent from Edinburgh when Rizzio and Darnley were murdered, and when Mary married Bothwell—the troubled months of 1566 and 1567. The second period of absence lasted from May 1571 to August 1572, when Kirkcaldy of Grange held

Edinburgh before 1560

Edinburgh Castle for the Queen, and had declared himself hostile to Knox. Knox was during the whole of this time minister of Edinburgh.

The kingdom was, as has been seen, for the fourteen years between 1558 and 1572 in a state of civil war, with religion as the nominal subject at issue between the factions; and the strife of the country at large was focussed in the capital. The city records of Edinburgh bear an eloquent though practical witness to the discords of the time. The "Extracts" published by the Scottish Burgh Records Society show that the Town Council was preparing early for the storm, and the passages already published might be largely supplemented on this point from the records still in manuscript. The entry of December 29th, 1557, runs as follows:—"The quhilk day the bailies, dean of guild, assessor, councillors, and deacons, being convenit in the Tolbuith of this burgh to the effect underwrittin, all with ane consent thinkis expedient and ordanis this town to be fortit strenthit and the wallis

John Knox & Edinburgh

thairof reparit in all places of the samin eftir the devyis and sicht of the personis eftir following, namit to that effect, that is to say:—Maister Thomas M'Calyeane [and nine others.]" The citizens requested on May 9th, 1558, that they should be given a governor in the absence of the Provost, Lord Seton, on account of "the present apperance of weris and invasioun of inimeis, and how that this said burgh wes desolait of ane superiour of jugement, knawledge, and habilite to haue the charge caire and reull of the samyn in case of invasioun as said is." The Council appointed on May 21, 1558, Robert Caldour and William Kelle "gunneris for thre monethis," and "Gilbert Balfour to be a maister of the townys artailye"; and ordered at the same time that the "futtis" or exits of the "closes" on both sides of the high street should be closed and built up with stone and lime "in case of invasioun of inimeis." The exits of the "wynds" or thoroughfares, as they may be regarded, were still to be left open. A muster of the citizens was also

Edinburgh before 1560

commanded that it might be known how many the Council could depend upon "for defence of this burgh."

It was ordered within a week after this (May 27) that all the town records and the silver work and ornaments of St Giles' should be taken to the Castle for safety, and that no one should leave the town lest they should be required to repel an enemy. Who the enemy was appears from the entry of June 5th, commanding every citizen to have his servant "sufficientlie prouidit for defence of this burgh in case the samyn be invadyt be our auld inimeis." This item from the Minutes shows that at that date the machinations of England were of no avail with the rulers of Edinburgh. It would seem, indeed, from the records generally that the better class of the citizens of Edinburgh had little sympathy in these early years with the principles that at last gained the upper hand, though they accepted them quietly enough when Mary had discredited her own cause. Religious affairs were in a state of chaos. The Church

John Knox & Edinburgh

of St Giles—the parish church of the town—was held at this time by the "Congregation." John Knox had been appointed "minister" on July 7th, 1559, apparently by a show of hands, and worship was celebrated in accordance with the Reformed rites. It had been agreed between the Queen's Commissioners and the Lords of the Congregation that a truce should be granted in religious matters in Edinburgh until January 10th, 1560, "swa that euery man may hawe fredome of his conscience vnto the said day." The Earls of Arran and Huntly and Lord Erskine appeared before the Town Council as a deputation from the Queen to propose that the question of which religion should be maintained unto that date should be submitted to a popular vote. But the reformers were in possession and were not inclined to accept the popular voice at this juncture, since "the maist pairt of men hes euer bene aganis God and his treuthe, at the leist hes nocht planlie embraced the samyn." They characterised the proposed plebiscite as "the voting of the wikkit," and their opposition

Edinburgh before 1560

was so strong that the Queen's representatives withdrew the proposal.

The Town Treasurer's accounts for these years when the old order in religious matters was giving way to the new have been recently printed, and give additional evidence of the disordered condition of Edinburgh, and the preparations for defence against an English invasion before the arrival of Knox gave the populace a leader. These accounts show also how quietly the Town Council accepted in 1560 the rule of the "Congregation" for the time. War with a foreign enemy was the one evil to be guarded against in 1557, 1558, and 1559, but in 1560 this danger had vanished through the temporary victory of the cause that had been looking for foreign aid. The following entries refer to the year 1557-58 :—

> Item to Robert Gray be ane speceall precept of the dait the vj Aprile, anno quo supra, throw the skayth sustenit be him throw the tramping doun of his herbis and distroying of his flowers and treis of his yaird be ane oppin passage to the biging of the walls of the toun, the sowme of .   iiij^{li}

John Knox & Edinburgh

Item be command of the presidentis, baillies, and Counsale to Maister Alexander Sym, advocat, for his labores and pynis takin in making of the Appellatioun in name and behalf of the saids Presidents, Baillies, Counsale and Corte, appeling frome the Bischop of Sanct Andrews monitors for non upputting of Sanct Geill[1] . . x^{li}

Item, the xxiiij day of Januare, gevin for ane gryt Slott to the Nether Bow, weyand xij^{li}, the price of the stane of maid wark xij^s ; summa is . . . . . ix^s

Item for twa silver culverings[2] to Michaell Gilbert to gif the young men occasioun to leir (learn) to schut with the culvering, price thairof . . . . . xl^s

Item, gevin to Thomas Coke, with the twa gunnars to pass to Bruntiland to vesy artailzerie twa syndrie tymes . . xiiij^s

Item, gevin for ane horss to Thomas Coke to

---

[1] This refers to the image of St Giles, which had been removed from its position in St Giles' Church, and had not been restored. "It was stolen during night-time in the month of July 1557, and was said to have been 'first drowned in the Nor' Loch, afterwards burnt.' The Archbishop ... appealed to the town, and as St Giles' day was approaching, when an effigy of the saint would be needed for the procession, he requested them 'either,' as John Knox in his History puts it, 'to get again the ald Saint Gile, or else on thair expenses to make a new image.' The council apparently refused to do either." "St Giles', Edinburgh," by J. Cameron Lees, D.D., LL.D., &c., 1889, p. 103.

[2] Long, slender pieces of ordnance.

Edinburgh before 1560

ryde to Dunbare and to Haymouth, for outserfing of bulletts . . . . x^s

Item, for an (blank) to hing the lok of the new wall upone . . . . . xij^d

A list is also given of the expenses

"maid upone the Butt at the Nether Bow in the moneth of Maij anno 1558, upone the bying of the Artailzerie and furnessing thairof, upone Johnne Morisonis two slangs (guns) with thair irne werk, and the expenses and bying of the four zetlings[1] coft[2] fra David Duf and James Litstair, and coft fra Johnne Bad ij brassin peces, preceidand the iiij day of September, anno 1558."

The same "dreadful note of preparation" is heard in the accounts for 1558-9.

The moanings of the storm that was to burst about the heads of the Regent and clergy had already been heard. The Minutes of Council and the general history of the time show that preparations were made to avert its violence if it came, though they proved of no avail. The jewels of St Giles' Church were weighed in December 1558 and in March 1559, and

---

[1] Cast guns. See "Council Records," July 27, 1576. [2] Bought.

John Knox & Edinburgh

ordered into safe custody. When the storm burst in the devastation of the religious houses in Perth on May 11th, 1559, a letter was sent by the Queen Regent to the Provost and Bailies directing that "ye fra thyne furthe gif gude heid and attendence that na sic vproir nor seditioun rys within your toun, bot that the religious places be surelie kepit." The Council took all proper precautions. A nightwatch was appointed for the church (June 21). The jewels and vestments were entrusted for safe keeping to certain named "honest men," "to be furth cumand and deliuerit be thame quhen thai suld be requirit thairto be the counsall" (June 27). "Thre score men of weyr" were "hyrit" (June 29) "for keping of Sanct Gelys Kirk and vphald of the stawis (stalls) of the queyr," and orders were given a fortnight later when the danger became extreme, that these carved stalls of the choir, which seem to have been regarded as of special value, should be removed for security to the Tolbooth. But in spite of Regent and Council the party of reform obtained the upper hand

Edinburgh before 1560

for a time, and on July 14th, two days after the order concerning the stalls, the sacred edifice was "purged of idolatrie" as far as possible "under the superintendence of the Earls of Argyll and Glencairn, and other leaders of the "Congregation." The victory, however, of the reformers was for the present only temporary. Reinforcements for the Queen Regent arrived from France on September 24th, and on November 9th the Church was again "purged," but this time from its "heretical pollutions," and re-consecrated by the Arch-Bishop of St Andrews. The vestments and ornaments were recovered from their custodiers, and mass was said within the walls of the church as before until its celebration finally ceased on March 31st, 1560.

The church itself was fortified during this disturbed period, as will be seen from the following extracts from the treasurer's accounts for the year:

Item, for rowing furth of the artaillzerie of
    the Flesche Markett .   .   .   .   v^s
Item, to xij men for rowing doun of v pece

John Knox & Edinburgh

to the Nether Bow, and bringing up of sex pece to the Provest huss	vj^s
Item, for laying of thre pece abone the Revestrie [1]	xij^d
Item xxv Maij for carrying of the artalzarie through the toun at ewyne	vj^s
Item xxvi maij, gewyne to foure werkmen for walking [2] of the artalzarie all nycht	iiij^s
Item xiiij day of Junij at the Quenis command to xxvij werkmen for drawin of the artalzarie upoun the gait,[3] to ilk ane of thame xvj^d	xxxvj^s
Item xxij Maij to George Tod for schoting of the said artalzarie	xxx^s
Item, for redding of the fulze [4] fra the Nether Bow bowt, to lay the slangis	xviij^d
Item xxij Septembris, to viij werkmen that laid furth the haill artalzarie furth of the Flesche huss to the Hie gait, and carying of two sclangis to the Greyfrier port, and uther twa to the blok huss at the Blak friers	vj^s
Item, foure Octobris, aucht werkmen for drawing of foure greit pece and thre cuthrollis [5] to the Stepill [6]	x^s viij^d

[1] The vestry of St Giles' Church. [2] Watching.
[3] Street, way, or road.
[4] Cleaning away the town filth. [5] Pieces of ordnance.
[6] The tower of St Giles, which was fortified for defence. The church was again held as a fortress by the partisans of the Queen in 1571-2.

Edinburgh before 1560

A list is then given of the expenses

"of the casting doun of the North Loche sensyne, taking furth of the red[1] of the ald wall, the beging[2] of the portis, wyndokis and durris of Leyth and Sanct Marie Wynd, precedand the iiij of Junij be the space of viij dayis, the expenses maid upoun the Kirk of Feild and Grey Freir Portis and the expenses of the North Loch wall and redding of the Fowsye[3] and biging up of certane sloppis [gaps] of the Freir yard, of new casting doun."

But the tone changes in 1560. The last mass had been said in March. Another party is in possession, and the town church must be altered to suit the change of taste. Altars and all their adornments were removed. Guns give way to pulpits, and the wages of soldiers are replaced by the "sustentation and furnessing of the ministers of this burgh."

Item the xxiij Apryle 1560, ressavit ane precept to content and pay to Johnne Inglis, massoun, for lyme and workmanschip of ane new powmpet[4] and ane lectroun and ane stoupe to hald the watter at the ministratioun of babtyme, the sowme of   .(blank)
Item xxiij Apryle 1560, ressavit ane precept

[1] Rubbish.   [2] Building.   [3] Ditch.   [4] Pulpit.

John Knox & Edinburgh

> to content and pay to James Baxter, wrycht, for the workmanschip of ane new powmpet and ane lectroun and ane stoupe to hald the watter at the ministratioun of baptyme, the sowme of . iiij[li]
> Item, the samyne day [8 May 1560] ressavit ane precept to content and pay to the honest sustentatioun and furnessing of the ministers of this burgh, the sowme of xl[li]
> Item xxv. Maij [1560] ressavit ane precept to content and pay to Mungo Hunter, smyth, for makin of thre keyis to the Kowgait Port, and for ane lok and ane ke to Johnne Knokis dur . . . xx[s]

This last item marks the completion of the first stage in the victory of the Reformation. Knox was no longer only the minister of the "Congregation." He was now minister of Edinburgh, and the Town Council of Edinburgh acknowledged the obligation of the citizens to support him as their minister, and to defray the expenses of the Reformed Establishment of religion within their bounds.

Payments made by the Town Council for John Knox and the Ministers

Payments made by the Town Council for John Knox and the Ministers

ONE of the most striking points of difference between the Edinburgh of Knox's time and the Edinburgh of to-day is the care that was exercised by the Town Council for the spiritual wants of the citizens. When the cause of reform gained at length the upper hand, the Council took upon itself, along with as much of the property of the old Church as it could get into its possession from time to time, the duty of dividing the revenues equitably between the Roman clergy and the ministers. The old Church had been disestablished and disendowed, but in Edinburgh, as elsewhere, it was held that its clergy should be granted a suitable maintenance. Two sets of ministers, in fact, were supported in the city in Knox's time, and, so far as appears, without objection from either side. It may be stated generally that specific endowments were continued to the Roman clergy, but that any sums payable out of the burgh funds were diverted to the new teachers of religion.[1]

The record still exists of the appointment of two new chaplains to altars in St Giles' Church on April 12th, 1559, and on August 4th "thankfull payment" was made to the prebendaries of St Giles "of all annuellis and dewiteis awin to thame in tymes begane." The break with the old order of things was not yet complete. Signs of change appear on February 16th, 1559-60. Three of the prebendaries and one chaplain are to receive

---

[1] "Though the stipends of the priests directly in the pay of the burgh were thus curtailed, they seem to have been otherwise unmolested in the enjoyment of their old revenues. They held the chaplaincies of the various altars to which they were attached to the time of their death, and drew the various annuals and pittances belonging to them. . . . Two instances may suffice. The provost of the church possessed a house in virtue of his office; this dwelling he was allowed to retain and finally to dispose of when it became uninhabitable." "St Giles', Edinburgh," by J. Cameron Lees, D.D., LL.D., 1889, p. 128.

Payments to Ministers

the usual payments; and the Treasurer is forbidden to disburse anything to the other prebendaries "becaus thai hawe nocht awatit vpone thair devyne service." A touch of irony may be felt in this reason for withholding payment, as it was impossible for the unfortunate prebendaries to discharge their duties at the time. The entry of October 15th, 1563, marks perhaps a temporary victory for the old faith. A priest, James Crawfurd, was ordered to produce "the rentell of the prebendariis rentis, and dewiteis quhilk pertenit to the queir," and the Council appointed another priest, John, or in the phrase of the time, Sir John Lithgow, to the benefice and prebendary of Craigcrook, which had fallen in by the decease of the former incumbent. But whatever may be the full statement of the case, it shows that the old system still survived. The storm was probably fiercer in the next year, 1564, when "Sir Jhonn Beyr," chaplain, renounced his yearly annual of £5 payable out of the common good, or, rather, commuted it

John Knox & Edinburgh

in view of the evil days that threatened for the sum of £27, 10s., "in full of said annuale."

Care was taken that nothing should be lost when the old Church finally went under. A record of all the monies that belonged to the prebendaries and chaplains, and of the annuals of the priests and friars was lodged in the Charterhouse in November 1565; and a collector was appointed in September 1567, "with awys [advice] and consent of Maister Jhone Craig, minister, and haill kirk of this burgh of Edinburgh," to whom minute and exhaustive instructions were given concerning the funds for which he would be held responsible. Yet the two orders of ecclesiastics must have existed curiously side by side. On March 3d, 1567-8, the Provost, Bailies, and Council, at the desire of the chaplain of St James' altar in St Giles' Kirk, consented, as patrons of that altar, that a tenement situated at the head of the Over Bow should be set in feu, the purchaser paying to the chaplain during his lifetime,

Payments to Ministers

"and efter his deceis to the hospitall foundit be the gude toune in the Trinitie College, the sowme twelf merkis yeirly feu maill." On April 7th of the same year the Bailies and Council, "efter consideratioun of the pouertie and auld decrepit age of Freir Andro Leis, blak freir," instructed the collectors of "the saidis freris renttis," to pay him yearly £16 during his lifetime. These examples show that the same spirit of fair dealing animated the Town Council of Edinburgh, which led the Parliament of 1567 to settle two-thirds of their incomes upon the ousted clergy for life. The Roman clergy continued also to occupy their old manses in St Giles' churchyard.

John Knox was appointed minister to the "Brethren of the Congregation" at a meeting held in the Tolbooth on July 7th, 1559. The position he was granted then was by no means secure, as he found it expedient to leave Edinburgh three weeks later, on July 24th. He seems to have been back in Edinburgh in April 1560, when a bond was drafted, possibly

John Knox & Edinburgh

by Knox himself, to consolidate the ranks of the Confederate Lords; and he took a leading part on July 19th, 1560, in a solemn thanksgiving in St Giles to commemorate a treaty signed on the 6th, by which the French troops were to be removed from the country. By this treaty England gained all that she could reasonably wish, and the Lords of the Congregation became practically the masters of Scotland. The Magistrates of Edinburgh accepted the situation at once, and treated Knox, as was complained of at the time, like a lord.[1] He was now the minister of Edinburgh in reality as well as in name.

The authorities for the financial side of Knox's connection with Edinburgh are primarily the manuscript records in the City Chambers. Extracts from them have been published by the Scottish Burgh Records Society. The Treasurer's and the Dean of

---

[1] The "curious comparison" was made that "there were many lords who had not so much to spend" as the Reformed clergy. Knox admits the justice of the comparison by implication in his "History." Hill Burton's "History of Scotland." Vol. IV., page 42.

Payments to Ministers

Guild's accounts for the years 1549 to 1567 have been printed recently by order of the Town Council. The manuscript minutes for this period have also been examined for the purposes of this investigation, and the entries of payments made to John Knox brought down to the latest date. The Treasurer's accounts introduce an expression under the date May 1560, which has been already quoted. It shows the kindly feeling of the rulers of that year toward the ministers, and is the precursor of many more of the same tenor—"ressavit ane precept to content and pay to the *honest sustentation* and furnessing of the ministers of this burgh the sowme of xl$^{li.}$"

The first reference in the Council minutes to any payments on account of the Reformed clergy occurs under date October 30th, 1560,—"the Prowest, Baillies, and Counsaill ordanis James Barroun to content and pay to John Knox the sowme of sax scoir poundis of the reddiest money of the townis being in his handis, and siklyk the sowme of xx$^{li.}$ for

John Knox & Edinburgh

irne and fyre werks furnesit and maid to his hous."

The items that refer to the payment of stipend to the new order of ecclesiastics follow each other after this in rapid succession. The next entry referring to Knox is that of December 20th, 1560, which refers to stipend alone, — "the Prowest, Baillies, and Counsall ordanis James Barroun to content and pay to Jhone Knox, minister, the sowme of fyftie pund money of this realme for the second termes payment, of the reddeist money that the said James hes in his handis of the gud townis." Orders were given on January 3rd, 1560-1, to pay forty pounds to John Cairns, who was reader in St Giles', "for his expenssis maid and service in tymes bigane;" on February 12th to pay to "John Knox, minister, the sowme of fyftie poundis for supporting of his chargeis;" on April 5th, 1561, "to deliver and pay to the minister, Jhone Knox, the sowme of fyftie poundis as for the compleit payment [for a quarter];" on April 24th "to deliver to John

Payments to Ministers

Carnys the sowme of ten pundis to ane compt of his dewtie for his service;" and on May 30th, "incontinent to deliver to Johne Knox, minister, the sowme of fyftie poundis, as for his quarter payment." The treasurer's accounts from Martinmas 1560 to Martinmas 1561, record a payment to John Knox of one hundred pounds out of the rental of the burgh mills:—

> Item maire givin to the said Jamis [Adamsoun] of the fermis of the common [milnis] to Johnne Knox, minister, as the said Jamis compt givin to me thairupon beris . jc^{li}

The entry of September 26th, 1561, identifies John Cairns, and gives orders as to his maintenance for the future—"the prouest baillies and counsale, vpoun consideratioun of the necessar and godlie seruice dailie done by Jhone Carnys, lectour of the mornyng prayeris, ordanis the collectouris of the taxt to deliver to the said Jhonne Carnys the sowme of thre score of pundis, in recompense and compleit payment of his seruice of all tymes bigane vnto the feist of Mychaelmes nixt; and

John Knox & Edinburgh

ordanis the collectouris of the annuellis appoyntit for the ministeris of the kirk to refound the said thre score of pundis agane to the saidis collectouris of the taxt, and forther in tyme cuming appoynttis yeirlie to the said Jhonne Carnys the sowme of ane hundredth merkis in the yeir of the radeast of the saidis annuallis, to be payit to him termelie as vse is, bigynnand at the said feist of Mychaelmes and to endure induring thair willis." Cairns received forty pounds again on November 8th.

The minute of June 19th, 1562, is a particularly interesting one for many reasons. The Town Council are found here electing a clergyman, and the citizens are to provide the needful funds for him and those whom he is to assist—"the prouest baillies counsale [and deacons of crafts] efter lang ressonyng vpoun the necessite of ministeris, fyndis that thair salbe ane vther minister electit be the prouest baillies and counsale dekynnis and eldaris, of this burgh, and adionit to Jhonn Knox minister, and for sustenyng of thame bayth, togidder with Jhonn Cairnys reder, ordanis the

Payments to Ministers

baillies, everyane within his awin quarter, to convene the merchanttis and requyre of everyane of thame quhat thay will quarterlie gyf for the caus foresaid; and siclike the saidis dekynnis to convene thair craftis, and report thair ansuerris vpoun Wednisday nixt."

On January 21, 1563-4, "the bailleis and counsale ordanis David Forster and Maister Jhonne Prestoun, collectouris for the ministeris, to deliver to Jhonne Carnys, reder, the some of xl^{li} of the radeast money in thair handis." Was the zeal of the citizens for reform cooling, or were the city funds low, that the hat, in popular language, was sent round on April 24th, 1564? [1]—"the baillies and remanent

[1] The cause of the Reformation was in imminent peril several times between 1560 and 1567. A formidable riot in July 1561 showed that the populace had not yet been won over. They broke out on account of the suppression of the games of Robin Hood, and, defying the Magistrates and Knox, who had refused to interfere, forced their way into the Tolbooth, and released one of their number who had been condemned to death, along with several other prisoners who were awaiting their punishment. "From the general tendency of affairs since Mary's arrival, the Catholic clergy were naturally encouraged to form good hopes for the near future. As the law stood, they were forbidden the public exercise of their religion; but the slackness of the Government had in some degree made the law a dead letter. During the Easter of 1563 the mass was celebrated in different

John Knox & Edinburgh

counsale befair writtin ordanis James Barroun, James Adamson, Maister Johne Prestoun, Eduard Hoipe, to pas out throuch the quarteris of the toun amangis the faithfull and require of every ane of thame quhat thae will frelie gif be yeir for sustening of the ministeris, and to report thair ansueris in writ vpoun the nixt counsale day." Stricter measures were taken within a fortnight—"May 3d, 1564—[the bailies and council] ordanis the haill communicantis to be convenit befoir thame vpoun Friday nixt, and first the northwest quartar,

parts of the country in such open fashion that the Protestants resolved on stringent measures" (Hume Brown's "Life of John Knox," II., 184). "In the Autumn of 1563 Knox took a step that seemed likely to put him at last in the Queen's power, and seriously to weaken his authority in the country" (Hume Brown's "Knox," II., 197). "In less than three months after her marriage [July 29th, 1565] Mary had beaten him [Moray] at all points, and triumphantly driven him and his associates across the Border to be further humiliated by a chilling reception at the English Court. In this ruin of the Protestant politicians, Knox must have had the grim satisfaction of seeing the fulfilment of his endless prophesying. These youths, who had first sat at his feet, and then scorned his counsels, had been taught who was the true interpreter of God's ways with His people. But if this feeling touched him, it was lost in the gloom of the new situation. As far as eye could see, the cause of true religion seemed at length to be fatally wrecked. Its most powerful friends were in exile, two Papist sovereigns sat on the throne, and Papists ruled all their councils" (Hume Brown's "Knox," II., 207, 208).

Payments to Ministers

and sa furth quarterlie that it may be sene quhat euerie ane of thame will frelie grant for sustening of the ministeris, and euerie baillie to convene his awin quarter." Fresh orders were issued on November 30th to the same effect—" the prouest, bailies, dene of gild, thesaurer and counsale, ordanis Robert Kar, Alexander Clerk, James Lowrye, and James Nichole, to travell amangis the faythful for collecting of the ministeris stepend, and to report ansuer to the counsale." A deputation from the craftsmen of the town appeared before the Council on January 2d, 1564-5, to undertake the care of their own poor and to remind the Council of its duties to the minister and the poor generally—" the prouest, baillies, and counsale and hale dekynnis, being convenit within the counsalhous of this burgh, comperit Jhonn Purves, dekin of the talyeouris, and for him self and remanent of the hale craftis oblist him and thame to sustene the hale pure of all occupatiounis within this burgh, sic as craftismen, craftis menis wyffis, seruandis and wedois, vpoun thair awin proper chargeis fra this day furth, sua that the gude toun nor nane resortand thairto salbe trublit with thair purys; and siclike, quhatsumever ordour salbe found gude be the prouest, baillies and counsale forsaid for sustenyng of the ministers, that they sall glaidlie beyr and deburse thair ressonabill pairt thereof at thair sychtis; and heirfor requestit the said prouest, baillies, and counsale to be mynderful of the saidis ministeris and pure, and in case they wantit thair ressonable charges that na falt war imput to thame heirafter."

The voluntary contributions of the "faithful" of April 24th, and of the "communicantis" of May 3d, had not proved a success, for in January we read "[the provost, bailies, council, and deacons of crafts] all in ane voce, consenttis granttis and ordanis that the haill inhabitantis of this burgh be set to certane particulare sowmes be the provest baillies and counsale, and the samyn to be upliftit and inbrocht quarterlie, to be distributit for sustenyng of the pure and sic as lauboris in publict service of the kirk, and till indure

Payments to Ministers

quhill vther remeid may be prouidit." The minute of March 12th, 1566-7, shows that some of the old funds had at last been released for the payment of the ministers,—"the quhilk day, deliverit, at the baillies and counsallis command, to Maister Jhone Craig, minister, the writting of the lordis of secreit counsall direct to the provest and baillies of this burgh for taking of ordaur and setting of taxt for sustening of thair ministerris, makand mentioun that hir grace had given the annuallis for that effect." These "annuals" were evidently the "vther remeid" that the Council had in view on May 3d of the previous year. Darnley had been murdered on the 9th of February, and we may read in this minute of March 12th the desire of Bothwell to secure to himself the Reformation party, a design in which he was "signally defeated."[1] The confederate Lords won the day at Carberry Hill and Langside, and the cause of the Reformation was at last fairly secure. Yet the remaining entries of this period show that however generous the inten-

[1] Hill Burton's "History of Scotland," IV., 212.

John Knox & Edinburgh

tions of the magistrates might be, there was sometimes considerable difficulty in securing money for the minister's stipends. John Knox is only mentioned in this later period in connection with the payment of his house rent or "maill." Orders were given on July 29th, 1569, that John Cairns should receive 16 marks for house rent in part payment of stipend still due, and the following significant record appears under the date of August 10th, " the counsale ordanis the baillies to put all sic personis in waird as ar decernit be decrete befoir the tovne's commissaris to pay the annuallis of thair landis to the hospital and ministrie, thair to remane vpoun thair awin expenses ay and quhill the said decreit be satefeit, and that becaus it is provin this day befoir thame be George Gourlay, officer, that he hes chairgit the said personis and thay refusit." A collector " for the ministrie " was appointed in this same month, August 1569.

Five entries are found in the printed minutes for 1570 which refer to stipend. A meeting of council was held on August 11th "for provisioun to be maid for Maister Jhone Craig,

Payments to Ministers

minister." Orders were given to the deacons of crafts on October 25th to convene the members of the crafts " and inquyre of thair benevolence quhat thai will geve to the support of the ministeris." The deacons reported to the council on November 1st " quhat ilk craft wald perfurnis and gif." The sums voted ranged from twenty shillings Scots on the part of the " wobstaris " or weavers to twenty pounds by the skinners, and the entries that cover the period of Knox's residence in Edinburgh end with the appointment at a meeting of Council on November 15th of " collectouris for procuring of the beneuolence of the godlie to the support of the ministaris stepend." A resolution of considerable historical interest had been passed in the meantime on August 24th. It marks another stage in the gradual diversion of the old revenues to the support of the ministers of the Reformed faith, but it shows also that the step referred to was not taken without some hesitation—" efter lang ressoning vpoun the ministeris stipend and how and quhair vpoun thai sall be sustenit, it is thocht guid be the baillies and counsall foirsaid that the auld dewtye quhilk wes payit be the inhabitantis of this burgh to the prouest vicare and clerk of the paroche kirk be collectit of new and appoyntit vpoun the said ministrie, and the saidis dekynis desyrit till awys with this quhill the morne, quhilk wes grantit." The extracts for this period close with the minute of May 1st, 1571.[1] After that there is a blank until 11th November 1573.

The Town Council did not limit its expenditure upon the ministers to the provision of stipend; it secured also houses for them and furniture to at least a considerable extent, and carried out all necessary alterations or repairs. The house-rent was generally paid through the treasurer; the furnishing and miscellaneous expenses in which Communion expenses were included, were defrayed by the Dean of Guild. The following extracts from the Treasurer's Accounts, 1559-66, refer specially to the payments of house-rent for John Knox himself:—

[1] See pages 49 and 131.

Payments to Ministers

Item, to Robert Mowbray for the Witsoundayis terme mail laist of ane ludgyn pertening to him in heritage, occupiit be Jhonne Knox, be ane precept of the dait the xxv day of August [1560-61] xxxv marks

Item to Robert Mowbray be ane precept of the date the xxv Februar [1561-2] xxv merks

Item, delyverit to Robert Mowbray, be ane precept of the dait the (blank) day of (blank), for the maill of his ludgyn quhilk Johnne Knox, minister occupiis   xxxiij^{li} vj^s viij^d

Item, the vij day of Mairche, [1563-64] resavitt ane preceptt to answer Androw Mowbray for the Mairtemes terme of the minister Jhonn Knox duelling hous . . . . . . xvj^{li} xiij^s 4^d

Item, the xvij day of Junij 1564 resavitt ane preceptt to answer Andrew Mowbray, the Witsonday terme of Jhonn Knox duelling houss; summa . . xvj^{li} xiij^s 4^d

Item to Robert Mowbray be ane precept for Jhonn Knox houss maill in the yeir of the comptaris office of the daitt threttie day of November jm. vc. lxiiij. yeris   xvj^{li} xiij^s

Item—Julij—be ane precept to answer Robert Scot for Jhonn Knox houss maill, daitit the xvj day of July 1565 yeris   xvj^{li} xiij^s iiij^d

Ane preceptt daititt the ix day of Januar, 1565-[66], to delyuer to Robert Scott, wrytar, for the mertimes maill of his

John Knox & Edinburgh

  hous, occupeitt be Jhonn Knox, minister,
   the soume of . . . . xxv marks
Ane preceptt, daititt the xxv day of September
  1566, to contentt and pay to Robert Scott,
  wrytar, and his spous, the soume of xxv
  marks for the Witsondayis termes mailes,
  1566, of the luging occupeitt be Jhonn
  Knox, minister; inde . . . xxv marks

These entries in the Treasurer's accounts can be supplemented at great length from the burgh records themselves. The first item is that of May 8th, 1560, which "ordanis Alexander Park, theasaurer, to delyver to Johne Carnis the sowme of xl^{li} for furnesching of thair minister, Johne Knox in his household, and because the said Johne Knox hes bene furnesit vpone Dauid Forresteris expenssis sen his coming to this toun be the space of 15 dayis lastbipast, ordanis the said Johne Carnis to ressave the said Dauid comptis and mak him payment of the sowmes debursit be him on the first end of the sowme of xl^{li} to be delyverit to him." It will be observed that this goes far beyond the payment of house rent alone. On August 16th the Treasurer

Payments to Ministers

was ordained to pay to John Carnis fifty pounds "for furnessing of the minister." This sum appears in the printed extracts as "fyue," but in the original transcript it is "fifty." Up to this time Knox had been accommodated in what would now be called "furnished lodgings," but an attempt was made at once to obtain for him a settled abode—" 4 September 1560, the Baillies and Counsaill, having consideratioun that, for the eis of Johne Knox minister, John Durie, talyeour, removit him furth of the ludging occupyit be the abbot of Drumfermeling, to the effect the said minister mycht enter thairto, ordanis Alexander Park, thesaurer, to content and pay to the said John Durie the sowme of viij merkis, and the samyn sall be allowit, &c.; and als the saidis baillies and Counsaill faithfullie promettis that how sone thai may provide the said minister ane vther ludgeing, to enter the said Johne to the possession thairof."

It appears from the item of February 12th, 1560-61, that John Knox was then settled in that house of Robert Mowbray's in which the

John Knox & Edinburgh

extracts from the Treasurer's accounts already given show that he was living in 1564,—"the treasurer to pay 'Robert Mowbray, heretour of the hous occupyit be Johne Knox,' ten merks, as the duty thereof to the preceding Martinmas, 'and fra thineforth to pay him termlie according to fyftie merkis in the yeir sa lang as the samyne sall be occupyit be him.'" Is there any curious story behind the entry of November 29th, 1564, or was it merely as a matter of form that the Treasurer was "ordained to mak gude and thankfull payment to Robert Mowbray of Johnne Knokis hous maill induring the tyme of his office, as vther thesauraris hes done of before." If it was only a formal entry, it is a little strange that two years later we find that the house which Knox occupied has changed ownership, and that he was compelled to engage a lawyer to claim his rent as he had himself been sued for it through non-payment,—"25th September 1566, the prouest [bailies and council] being convenit for chesing of the new counsall, compeirit Jhone Johnstoun, writer, declarand

Payments to Ministers

that John Knox, minister, had written to him that he wes craiffit, at the leist sutit, for his Mertymes termes maill, in the yeir of God jm. vc. and lxv. be Robert Scottis spous, desyrit thair wisdomes outher to caus the samyn be payit, other wayis it behuiffit him to find the way to satiffie the samyn." It is satisfactory to find that the treasurer was ordained to make payment of the sum craved. But what had happened by February 20th, 1567-8, when the treasurer was ordained "to deliver to Mungo Bradie, goldsmyth, cautinare and suertie for Jhone Knox hous maill, the sowme of x merkis?" Shall we read the entries as proofs of what we know from other sources that the cause of the Reformation was still hanging in the balance and that very little would at this time have turned the scale the other way, when the Reformer himself was processed for house rent and his cautioner or surety was compelled to pay?

Knox had changed his residence before November of this year, but his troubles still continued. The treasurer was commanded on

John Knox & Edinburgh

the 19th of that month "to caus mend and repair the necessaris of Jhone Knox dwelling hous, vpoun the expenssis of Johne Adamsoun and Bessie Otterburne his spous, conjunct fear thairof, and deduce the samyn of thair hous maill, becaus thai haif bene aft tymes requyrit to do the samyn and refussit." The repairs referred to were carried out exactly as such repairs would be carried out in similar circumstances to-day,—" March 4, 1568-9. The bailies and counsell ordanis Andro Stewinsoun, thesaurer, to pay to Jhone Adamesoun the sowme of fourty merkis for the maill of his hous occupeit be Jhone Knox the yeir past, deduceand thairof the sowme of aucht pund debursitt be the said thesaurar in reparalyng of the said hous in defalt of the said Jhone Adamsoun, being requyrit to do the same, and als xij merkis xij^s debursit mair be the said thesaurar in repairing of the samyn hous by the viij^{li} above mentionat debursit be the said Jhonn."

The last entry in the Council Records referring to John Knox's house rent is that

Payments to Ministers

given in the Manuscript Minutes under date November 23rd, 1569—"the quhilk day the Baillies and Counsale ordanis Thomas Henrison treasurer to deliver John Adamson the sum of twentie markis for the Mertymes male of John Knox's house and the same salbe allowit in his comptis." Knox left Edinburgh for St Andrews in May 1571, and returned towards the end of August 1572. He died in the November following. No entry appears in the minutes to guide us as to where he lived during these three months. In all probability no minutes of Council were taken or entered during that unsettled period of practically civil war.

The Dean of Guild's accounts for the early years of Knox's ministry give elaborate particulars of the pains that were taken to secure his well-being in other respects. As early as May 15th, 1560, the Treasurer was ordered by the Council to supply "ane lok to John Knox ludgeing." The Dean of Guild supplied him with "ane Frenche lecteron buk" about October 15th, at a cost of twenty shillings. On October 18th he paid for "lokkis, bandis,

John Knox & Edinburgh

and [blank] to the minister's ludging," and defrayed the slater's expenses "for poynting ane parte of his house and cleinging gutters." These payments were natural enough, but, descending to more minute particulars, we find the Dean accounting on December 22d "for ane lok to Jhoun Knox yet [gate] and twa keyis," "for mending ane throwch lok and ane new key," and "for putting in of ane stepill to his chek lok, and leid." Selecting a few more of these items from the palmy days when the cause of reform was enjoying a foretaste of success, and the Town Council of Edinburgh was open-handed, we find that in January 1560-61, payments were made "to the Glaschinwrycht for xij fute of new glass to John Knox xviij^d the fut, summa xliiij^s;" that there was purchased in April 1561 "xij dressit daillis to Johnne Knox study," and "xiij uther daillis to Johnne Knox study;" and that between October 1560 and 1561 an account of eighteen shillings was paid "for ane moudewall and ane lok to Johnne Knox study." The study seems to

Payments to Ministers

have been still unsatisfactory in spite of these repairs, as on November 5th, 1561, the Dean of Guild was ordered "with all diligence to mak ane warme studye of daillis to the minister, Johnne Knox, within his lugeing, abone the hall of the samyne, with lychtis and wyndokis thairto, and all uther necessaris."

An exhaustive list of the expenses incurred in the construction of this study is preserved in the Dean of Guild's accounts. A "poor man" received eight shillings for removing rubbish. Stones were carried from the churchyard at the cost of sixpence, "to be soill, lintell, and vtheris necessaris to the said windo." It cost thirteen shillings to saw "ix gestis and twa daillis to the said studie." Three dozen "doubill garroun" nails and some "plancheaur" nails cost four shillings. Candles cost ninepence. "To Johnne Cunnynghame and Johnne Melross, wrychtis, and ane servant with thame, for ane oulk and iij dayis labouris, viz., to the said Cunnynghame in the oulk xxvij^s, to the said Melrose xxiiij^s, and thar servand xxij^s, summa togidder

John Knox & Edinburgh

iiij^{li} xvj$^{s.}$." Item mair, the said awld middle wall cuttit and the tymmer thereof sawin for makinge entrees fre the ministeris chalmer to the study, for naillis to the standartis, stappis, bilzeittis of the entre therto, vij^s iiij$^{d.}$." "Item, mair for candill ix$^{d.}$." "Item, for ane lok and key and snek within to the said study dur." Forty shillings was paid to Patrik Schange and his servants "for making of lange skelffis and letteronis and saittis in the ministeris study, be the space of aucht dayis." He received also thirty shillings for designing and making "ane greit foure square lettrane [desk] to the ministeris, turneand upon ane wyce" [vice]. The exceptional nature of this desk is quaintly implied in the wording of the item, from which it appears that this sum of thirty shillings included an allowance "for troubling of his spreit in the inventing of that consait." The "lettrane" was furnished with a "loke and bandis" at the cost of six shillings. The accounts for 1562 afford also a passing glimpse of some of the ordinary discomforts of civilised life:—

Payments to Ministers

"Item, to the ministeris lugeing being falthie in diverss pairtis of the sklattis tharof and the rane comand done abone his bed and buikis, for pointinge of the samin haill throche xxiiij[s]."

It is plain from numerous entries in the Council minutes that John Knox was not specially favoured in these matters. A few of these may suffice for this purpose. Three items in the Treasurer's Accounts for 1559 are as follows, and relate to the "ministers," by which we are to understand the preachers of the "Congregation," who had come to Edinburgh along with the Lords in that year:—

Item, the first Junij ressavit ane precept to content and pay to Johnn Carnis for furnissing of Johnne Willokis and remanent of the ministers . . . xx[li]

Item the xxvj Junij ressavit ane precept to content and pay to Johnn Carnis for furnessing of the ministers, the sowme . lx[li]

Item xxvj August ressavit ane precept to content and pay to Jhonn Carnis for furnessing of the ministers; summa . l[li]

John Knox & Edinburgh

John Willock, or Willocks, officiated in St Giles' instead of Knox during part of 1559, when Knox was compelled to retire from Edinburgh on account of the arrival of the Queen-Regent. He celebrated communion in St Giles' according to the Reformed rite in August 1559, probably the first occasion on which it was done. The Regent, Mary of Lorraine, accepted his ministrations on her death-bed on June 10th, 1560. Orders were given on August 30th, 1560, that Willock should receive "xxti crownis of the sone,[1] for recompans of the greit travell sustenit be him

[1] The "crowns of the sun" were French gold pieces, the value of which varied considerably during the sixteenth century. In 1523 a "crown of the sun" was worth twenty shillings and threepence Scots; in 1555, twenty-three shillings and sixpence; and in 1582, fifty shillings (Cochran-Patrick's "Coinage of Scotland"). The extract from the Treasurer's accounts given in the text settles the value of a "crown of the sun" in 1560 as one pound six shillings and eightpence Scots. The only similar piece in the Scottish coinage is the unique gold crown of Mary, dated 1561, which has the sun for mint mark. Any "crowns of the sun" current in Scotland before 1560 were of French minting; after 1561, they may have been coined either in Scotland or France. Kenyon states in his "Gold Coins of England" that in 1522 and 1525, in consequence, it must be presumed, of the insufficiency of the English coinage, foreign coins both of gold and silver were proclaimed current in England. Every crown of gold not soleil (*i.e.* not being a French crown of the sun), nor clipped,

Payments to Ministers

this haill yere bigane in preching and ministering of the sacramentis within this burgh; and [the minute] ordanis ane member of the counsaill to thank him for his greit beneuolence for the greit travaill foresaid"[1] It is this same twenty "crowns of the sun" that are referred to in the following extract from the treasurer's accounts for this year :—

Item, xx September, ressavit ane precept to
    content and pay to Robert Watson, xx
    crownis of the sonn to be deliverit be
    him to Jhonn Willokis ; summa xxvj^{li} xiij^s iiij^d

This was in the opening days of the Reformation. It was the same in later years. Two entries in the Dean of Guild accounts for 1565 show that in the minor details referred

was ordered to pass in 1522 for four shillings, and every "crown soleil of weight" in 1525 for four shillings and fourpence sterling.

[1] Willock was a prominent figure of the time. He was the principal coadjutor of Knox in the early stages of the Reformation. He took part, along with Knox and others, in the preparation of the "Confession of Faith" of 1560, and the "First Book of Discipline." He was appointed "Superintendent" of Glasgow, an office created under the provisions of the "First Book of Discipline," but he did not hold the office for long. He was an Englishman, and returned voluntarily to England, where he held the rectory of Loughborough.

John Knox & Edinburgh

to in the preceding paragraphs, all the Reformed clergy shared in the generosity of the Council. The Town Council considered it their duty to attend not only to the necessities but also to the comforts of all teachers of the new faith. —"item, 8 Nov. 1565. For tua braid dailes quhilk I coft[1] and gaif to Maister Jhonn Craig, minister, the quhilk he desyritt to mak skelfis and lettronis to his buikis, pryce of pece v^s $iiij^d$; somme x^s $viij^d$."—"Item, for baring of thame fra Leyth to the said Maister Jhonis hous, $viij^d$." This John Craig had been minister of the Canongate, but was induced about 1563 to become colleague to Knox in St Giles'. It will be remembered, on the other hand, as against this generosity on the part of the Council, that very considerable difficulty was experienced in procuring stipends during these years. The statement is made in one place, June 11, 1563, that a collection was ordered for John Craig and John Cairns, since they had received nothing for a half-year past, and the items concerning the shelves and

[1] Bought.

Payments to Ministers

desks may be interpreted as another proof that in general the Council seems to have been more favourable to the cause of the Reformation than the bulk of the citizens, who had to pay the cost.

The following items, selected from amongst many others of similar import, show the attention that was given by the Town Council to miscellaneous ecclesiastical matters. They were not content in the earlier years of religious agitation with defraying the expenses of their "minister" when at home, but they took upon themselves also the charge of his disbursements when deputed on business of the "Kirk."—"December 31, 1561, the prouest, baillies, and counsale, vnderstanding that the minister, Jhonne Knox, is requyrit be the hale kirk to pas in the parttis of Angus and Mernys for electing of ane superintendent thair, to the quhilk thay thame selffis hes granttit, thairfor ordanis Alexander Guthre, dene of gild, to pas in cumpanye with him for furnessing of the said ministerris charges, and to deburse and pay the samyn of the radeast of the townis guddis in his handis, quhilk salbe allowit in his compttis, and forther to haist the said minister hame that the kirk heir be nocht desolait." It appears from the Dean of Guild's accounts that John Knox was absent from Edinburgh eleven days on this business, and that payments were made on behalf of himself and two servants and three horses to the amount of twenty pounds, fifteen shillings. John Knox and John Craig were deputed on a similar errand in 1564, and the Town Council of Edinburgh defrayed all charges as before,— "18 August 1564, the prouest [bailies and council] vnderstanding that be the command of the kirk Johnne Knox and Johnne Craig, ministeris, ar instantlie to depairt, the tane to the north and the vther to the south pairttis preiching of the evangell in tha pairttis, and that it is appoynttit that Christopher Gudeman, minister of Sanct Androis, sall abid and remane in thir pairttes to thair returnyng, and in thair places to minister and preche; quhairfor they ordane Jhonn Spens [and four others] to pass to the said Maister Gudman, offer him in

Payments to Ministers

thair names all honorable intertenement, and caus the stewert of Jhonne Knox hous to keip table to him vpoun the townis expenssis, and ordanis the said Alexander Park [the treasurer] to pay the samyn ouklie." Twenty pounds were paid on behalf of Goodman[1] under this order in September. The Dean of Guild's accounts for 1563-1564 speak of a journey contemplated by Knox through Merse, Teviotdale, and Nithsdale; and record a payment of three pounds to John Chalmers, "servand to the said minister," who was sent to St Andrews to ask that Goodman should be permitted to remain in Edinburgh until Knox's return, as the Council had been informed that he was to make a protracted tour through the southern districts mentioned. The Council elected, on the 18th of June 1563, two commissioners or, in modern phraseology, "representative elders," to attend the

---

[1] Willock, Goodman, and Knox were the challengers in a discussion held on the principles of the old faith before the Convention of 1561. Goodman had been colleague to Knox at Geneva in 1555. He also, like Willock, returned to England, his native country, where he died at Chester in 1601.

John Knox & Edinburgh

forthcoming General Assembly at Perth [Sanct Jonistoun] in company with John Knox. They appointed a master of the High School in 1568, and in the exercise of their general superintendence of both educational and ecclesiastical matters they issued an order on February 11th 1568-69, when the new master [Thomas Bucquhannane] was about to enter on his duties, that "the minister" should "publische the samyn to the pepill." The Town Council had in the meantime taken a bolder step than usual, in 1565, out of consideration for the Reformers. Mary and Darnley had requested that Knox should be silenced during their stay in the capital. Knox had offended Darnley by a sermon preached in St Giles' on August 19th. The minute of August 23d in that year contains the record of the emphatic refusal of the Council to obey their Majesties. Instead of muzzling Knox, they exhorted him to persevere,—"all in ane woce concludis and deliveris that thai will na maner of way consent or grant that his mouth be closit or he dischargeit in preiching the trew word, and

Payments to Ministers

thairfor willit him at his plesour, as God sould move his hart, to proceid fordwardt in trew doctrine as he hes bene of befoir, quhilk doctrine thai wald approve and abide at to thair lifis end." It would appear, however, that Knox's preaching must have ceased for a time, as Craig, his colleague, desired assistance "in respect he was alone."[1]

[1] Calderwood, II., 340.

Houses occupied by John Knox
in Edinburgh

Houses occupied by John Knox in Edinburgh

THE first reference to any house provided for the use of John Knox in Edinburgh is to be found in the minute of Council dated May 8, 1560, "the provost, ballies, and counsall ordanis Alexander Park, thesaurer, to delyuer to Johne Carnis the sowme of xl^{li} for furnesching of thair minister John Knox in his household, and becaus the said Johne Knox hes bene furnesit vpone David Forresteris expenssis sen his cuming to this toun be the space of xv dayis lastbipast; ordanis the said Johne Carnis to ressave the said David comptis, and mak him payment of the sowmes debursit be him on the first end of the sowme of xl^{li} to be delyuerit to him." The Dean of Guild's accounts for the period May to October 1560 contain also the following item, " to Margaret,

John Knox & Edinburgh

his barne[1] [Hepburn], the relict of umquhill Patrik Irland, for the said Johnis howss maill at the heving [leaving?] thereof x marks." On the 15th of May in this same year, 1560, the treasurer was ordered to pay for "ane lok to Johne Knox ludgeing."

A difficulty arises at this point as to how many houses are indicated in these references to payments. There might possibly be three, there are almost certainly two, but there might only be one. It is quite permissible to interpret them, in the absence of further identification, as applying to the separate houses of Cairns, Forrester, and Ireland. It is equally permissible to assert that Cairns had made provision for Knox being lodged in Ireland's house at Forrester's expense. The dates would authorise such a supposition, but the probabilities and the natural interpretation of the Council minute are against it.

The minute of June 1st, 1560, by which the treasurer was ordained " to delyuer to Johne

---

[1] This curious mistake was made by the clerk when transcribing the accounts in 1560.

Houses occupied by John Knox

Carnis the sowme of xx^{li} for furnesing of Johne Willok, precher," is one amongst several that would seem to indicate that Cairns, who held the position of "Reader" in St Giles, was also the agent through whom payments were generally made on account of the ministers. The entries, interpreted in this light, refer to him rather as paymaster than as what, in modern parlance, would be described as a "keeper of furnished apartments."[1] As regards Forrester, however, the case is different. It was in his house that Lord Seton, who was Provost of Edinburgh in 1558-59, was lodged, and his expenses were defrayed by the Council. The minute of September 2nd, 1559, which orders these expenses to be paid, indicates that Lord Seton resided there from Whitsunday until August. Forrester's house would thus be naturally regarded by the Council as a fitting abode for Knox when he arrived in

---

[1] Hume Brown takes the other view. "For the next few months Knox has a new landlord, John Cairns, whose name appears twice in the Records as the recipient of the minister's rent" ("Life of John Knox," II., 316). The statement in the text accords better with what is known of Cairns.

John Knox & Edinburgh

Edinburgh in 1560, or at least until a more permanent residence could be secured. Shortly before Knox's death, Forrester's house was still a place in which a visitor to the Scottish capital whom the authorities wished to honour could find a lodging suitable to his rank. The "Diurnal of Occurrents," Part II., p. 326, states that when Killigrew, the Ambassador of Queen Elizabeth, arrived at Edinburgh to congratulate the Earl of Morton on his accession to the Regency, he "depairtit to David Forrestaris lugeing above the Tolbuith."

David Forrester was a Bailie of Edinburgh, and a member of one of the old patrician families of the burgh. Adam Forrester was "Alderman" or Provost in 1373. His descendants became the Lord Forresters of Corstorphine, and were the founders of its ancient collegiate church. Forrester's Wynd had its name from them, and it was here that David Forrester lived. This wynd ran from the High Street to the Cowgate, and opened on the High Street on the spot where the Buccleuch statue now stands. Almost opposite

Houses occupied by John Knox

Forrester's Wynd, but a little farther to the west, was the entrance to Ireland's Close, named, as was the custom of the time, from a family of Ireland or Irland who resided there. Their house was at the bottom of the close, and stood on a spot opposite the south-east corner of the Bank of Scotland which is now occupied by the houses of St Giles Street. This close was afterwards called Dunbar's Close, changing its name, as was the common practice, with its owner. A sasine of February 1, 1754, records that at that date three generations of Dunbars had owned property here. Popular tradition asserted that it was given the new title because houses in it were occupied by the victors after the battle of Dunbar, and a house in the neighbouring close was pointed out as the residence of Cromwell himself, but sober history must record the more prosaic reason.

As far back as 1536 (November 21) sasines bear witness to a tenement in this locality which had been possessed by "the late John Ireland," and the property can be traced through sasines of 1538 (May 28), 1538-9 (March 3), 1540 (November 4 and 13), 1541 (August 19 and December 23), 1543 (December 20), to 1543 (December 21), when a tenement here came into possession of Patrick Ireland, son of the late John Ireland and Margaret Hepburn, his spouse, by resignation from David Ireland, "son and heir of the said late John," who was seized in the property on the same date by assignation from his mother and her second husband. David possessed already what had been apparently the front portion of his father's property abutting on the High Street.

The property of Patrick Ireland is identified (Dec. 21, 1543) as being bounded by "a tenement and lands respectively of John Arbukill and Robert Adamson on the west, the North Loch on the north, and the waste backland of the said tenement on the south, and the tenement and lands respectively of the heirs of the late James M'Calzeane and the late Walter Young on the east." The identification of property from a description

Houses occupied by John Knox

of 1543 might possibly be open to challenge as vitiated by the burnings of Edinburgh in 1544 and 1545, but a sasine of Oct. 22, 1551, identifies the tenement by practically the same boundaries—"tenement of Patrick Ireland burgess on the north side of the High Street, between a tenement of Mr Thomas Makcalzeane on the east, a tenement of the late John Arbukle and the late Robert Adamson on the west, and the North Loch on the north." Thomas Makcalzeane had become proprietor on September 4th, 1551, of the half of the property of Walter Young referred to in the sasine of 1543. This makes the descriptions of 1543 and 1551 identical. It appears from another sasine of 1551 (July 31), and a sasine of April 13, 1552, that Patrick Ireland was a bailie at that time. His ownership of the property described can be traced further through sasines of January 12, 1552-3, and March 30, 1554, until he is referred to in connection with the ownership of the same and surrounding properties as " the late Patrick

John Knox & Edinburgh

Ireland" on April 1st, 1559. But his name had not quite disappeared from the neighbourhood in 1754, when in the sasine of February 1st, already referred to, the tenement in question was described as situated "at the end or foot of the close of old called Ireland's Close, now Dunbar's Close."

The next item that refers explicitly to any particular house as retained for John Knox is that in the Council minutes for September 4th, 1560,—"the ballies and counsaill, haveing consideratioun that, for the eis of Johne Knox, minister, Johne Durie, talyeour, removit him furth of the ludgeing occupyit be the abbot of Drumfermeling to the effect the said minister mycht enter thairto, ordanis Alexander Park thesaurer to content and pay to the said Johne Durie the sowme of viij merkis, and the samyn sall be allowit, etc.; and als the saidis ballies and counsaill faithfullie promittis that how sone thai may provide the said minister ane vther ludgeing, to enter the said Johne to the possessioun thairof." No other item has yet been dis-

Houses occupied by John Knox

covered that can help to identify the "abbot of Drumfermeling's ludgeing." Wherever it was, it was clearly intended that the occupation should only be temporary. A comparison of dates would indicate that it might either be Patrick Ireland's house already referred to, or another house in which John Knox was residing five months later, but in any case his occupation of Ireland's house and of this, if it be a separate house, was in each case of very short duration.

The next item in order, that of February 14th,[1] 1560-61, brings us to Knox's first settled residence in Edinburgh, if it again should not be identified with the house that Durie vacated. The treasurer was ordered on that date to pay "Robert Mowbray, heretour of the hous occupyit be Jhone Knox . . . the sum of x merkis as for the dewtie thairof the tyme the samyne wes occupyit be the said Johne to the fest of Mertymas last and fra thinefurth to pay him termelie according to fyftie merkis in the yeir so lang as

[1] In the printed extracts this is February 12th.

John Knox & Edinburgh

the samyne sall be occupyit be him." This extract shows that a fifth part of a year's rent was paid for the time that Knox occupied this house before Martinmas 1560. Allowing that sum for the broken period of two months, it brings the date of Knox's entry very close to September 4th, on which day he was clearly living in Durie's house. The evidence, however, in favour of the identification of Mowbray's house with Durie's is not conclusive, as it is quite possible, though it can hardly be said probable, that the Council may have succeeded in renting Mowbray's house as a permanent residence for Knox within a few days of the passing of the minute of September 4. The phraseology of that minute, on the other hand, scarcely points to an occupation of Durie's house that was to extend to over six years.

The Council records show that rent was ordered to be paid for Mowbray's house on February 12, 1560-61, November 29, 1564, "as other thesavraris hes done of before," and September 25, 1566. It was, therefore, in

Houses occupied by John Knox

this house that the "warm study of deals" was erected, which has always been so prominent in the popular accounts of John Knox. The order to build it, which was given to the Dean of Guild on November 5th, 1561, was one of the few items from the Council Records referring to Knox that had become public property:—"with all deligence to mak ane warme studye of daillis to the minister, Jhonne Knox, within his lugeing abone the hall of the samyn, with lychtis and wyndokis thairto and all vther necessaris." It was in this house that Knox's first wife, Marjorie Bowes, died in the close of the year 1560, and it was to this house that Knox brought his second wife, Margaret Stewart, in 1564, a girl of seventeen. It was here also that Knox entertained the Duke of Chatelherault and the English resident Ambassador Randolph at the historical supper party of the last Sunday in November 1562, when Knox did his best to secure the adhesion of the Duke to the side of the English and the Reformers.

The history of the property on which

John Knox & Edinburgh

Mowbray's house stood has been traced back in the protocol books to before 1539. The names of two John Browns, father and son, are prominent in the title-deeds that refer to it. John Brown, the father, had possessed the whole strip of land with the buildings upon it, that extended from the High Street to the North Loch. John Brown, the son, would seem to have been the owner only of the portion that fronted the High Street. This John Brown, the younger, was executed in the year 1539 as a heretic in virtue of a sentence pronounced by Cardinal Beaton, and his house in the High Street was granted on the forfeiture of his properties to a Mr James Foulis of Colinton, Clerk of the Rolls. The "backlands" extending from this house to the North Loch are found in possession of Elizabeth Carkettill in the year of this John Brown's death. She, with the consent of her husband, Adam Stewart, resigned this property on September 23 in this same year to her three daughters, Katherine Hopper, Janet Hopper, and Helen Stewart, and their husbands, with

Houses occupied by John Knox

the exception of a small portion at the extreme north end, bounded by the North Loch, and extending 5¼ ells from north to south, which she had disposed of to Thomas Chisholm and Helen Napier his spouse. The first-named of the three daughters was married to Andrew Mowbray. On November 22, 1549, George Lundy, son of Helen Stewart and David Lundy, became seized of the third of the property that had passed to his mother, and he executed a resignation of this on the same date to Katherine Hopper, described as the relict of the foresaid Andrew Mowbray. On May 4, 1555, Robert Mowbray, son of Katherine Hopper, obtained possession of the whole property that had passed from Elizabeth Carkettill to her daughters, by seizin of his late father's third part of his mother's share, and of the third that belonged to Janet Hopper, described as relict of Mr Hugh Rigg.

It appears from the Protocol Books of Alexander Guthrie, Town-clerk of Edinburgh, that an instrument of sasine was expede on April 8th, 1563, in favour of Robert Mowbray, son and heir of the late Andrew Mowbray, and Jonet Cant his future spouse, in certain properties on both the north and south sides of the High Street, including that already referred to in the sasine of 1555.[1] The description of this latter property is interesting, as it is more particularly identified by being the residence of John Knox,—"thereafter the said Bailie (Andrew Sklater) passed to a tenement of land of the late John Brown, lying on the north side of the said burgh, between a tenement of land of David Fernelie on the east and a tenement of land of Robert Hopper on the west and there the said Robert (Mowbray) resigned, by delivery of earth and stone into the hands of the said Bailie, All and whole his great mansion and building, together with the garden and tail of the same now inhabited by John Knox, minister, with their pertinents, lying within the said tenement between the North Loch on the north and the foreland of the said tenement on the south."

[1] The properties already belonged to Mowbray. They were now, in accordance with custom, settled jointly on himself and his future wife.

Houses occupied by John Knox

A progress of titles connecting Mowbray's sasine with the title of the present proprietors of the greater portion of the ground, who are the Corporation of Edinburgh, has been made out partly from the protocol books of the various Town-clerks and partly from existing titles. From these the exact situation of the subjects contained in Mowbray's sasine can with certainty be ascertained.

The first link in the progress after Mowbray's sasine is a sasine of date March 28, 1565, in favour of Robert Scott, one of the clerks of the Lords of Council, and Elizabeth Scott, his spouse, proceeding on a resignation by Robert Mowbray and his spouse "of the backlands of the said Robert Mowbray, built and waste, under and above, with garden, tail, waste, porch, close, and transe thereof, having ish and entry by the front and by the back, lying within a tenement of the late John Brown, burgess, on the north side of the High Street, between a tenement of land of the late David Fairlie on the east, and a tenement of the late Robert Hopper on the west, the foreland of the

John Knox & Edinburgh

said tenement on the south, and a certain piece of tail of the said lands pertaining to the heirs of the late Thomas Chisholm, lying beside the North Loch, on the north." It will be noticed that this latter boundary—that by the late Thomas Chisholm's "piece of tail" on the north, carries back the identification to the resignation executed by Elizabeth Carkettill on September 23d, 1539.[1] The Contract of March 24th, 1564-5, in pursuance of which this sasine of 1565 was effected, identifies the property further as inhabited by John Knox—" the samyn and all their pertinentis now inhabet be Johnne Knox, minister of Edinburgh, lyand within the burgh of Edinburgh, on the north syd of the Hie Streit thairof, within the tenement of umquhile Johnne Broun, betuix the foirland of the said tenement at the south pairte, and the Pece Taill of land pertening to the airis of umquhile Thomas Chisholme on the north pairte, with the Yet, Throchgand, and Enteres thairto, and all utheris thair per-

[1] As showing the persistence of these old boundaries this "piece of tail" of Chisholm's is found referred to regularly as late as 1678 (May 20).

Houses occupied by John Knox

tenintis; quhilk Tenement of umquhile Johnne Broun lyis in the said burghe, on the north Pairte of the Hie Streit thairof, betuix the tenement of umquhile Farnlie on the east pairte, and the tenement of land (of) umquhile Mr Richard Hopper on the west pairte."

With this full identification of the property in question, there is no necessity for entering so minutely into the particulars of its history since 1565. Mr Robert Scott, son of the Robert Scott, clerk of Session, was infeft in the subjects on September 23d, 1568, and to him succeeded his son, John Scott, in 1593 (March 30) (designed in a later sasine as Mr John Scott[1] of Tarvet), who sold the property in 1612 (Dec. 10) to Thomas Speir, merchant, burgess of Edinburgh. On the death of Thomas Speir, his three daughters succeeded (1616, Dec. 28.) to the property, and on one of them dying a few years later the other two became pro indiviso proprietors of one-half each. In 1629 (May 1st), Rachael Speir, one

[1] The title "Mr" implies that he had proceeded to the University Degree of Master in Arts.

of the surviving daughters of Thomas Speir, and then wife of John Jackson, alienated her half to Thomas Charters, merchant. Process of division followed in 1630, and the property was divided up between Thomas Charters and Sarah Speir, who was the other surviving daughter of Thomas Speir, and is described in the sasine to her that followed the proceedings on July 1st, 1631, as "relict of Mr Robert Foullis, advocate." The position of Mowbray's property becomes localised in more modern terms in the sasine to Charters (1630, April 29) as bounded by "Bruce's Close on the West."[1] Henry Charters, son of Thomas Charters, succeeded to his father's portion of the subjects, and alienated it to Sir James Hope of Hopeton, Knight, one of the Senators

[1] A Sasine of January 25, 1566, and previous Sasines give the origin of the name "Bruce's Close." Robert Bruce of Binning granted in that year 24 marks yearly out of his "Backland" to Thomas M'Calzeane of Cliftonhall, Advocate, the same who is referred to frequently in the text. This "Backland" is described as bounded on the east by "a tenement of the late —— Carkettill, now pertaining to Robert Scott, writer,"—the tenement in which John Knox lived. Bruce's Close has been better known for more than two hundred years as Warriston (or Warriston's) Close. It ran between the properties owned in 1566 by Bruce of Binning and Scott.

Houses occupied by John Knox

of the College of Justice, sasine in whose favour was recorded 13th October 1652. The other portion of the subjects also fell into the hands of the Hopeton family, and in 1686 (Sep. 29) Charles Hope of Hopeton alienated the whole subjects to Alexander Abercrombie, vintner. In this sasine the property is again referred to as bounded by "the close called Bruce's Close on the west." Abercrombie appears soon afterwards to have got into difficulties, and Robert Watson, one of his creditors, obtained from the Court of Session on December 1, 1694, a "decreet of vendition and alienation" of the subjects in his favour. That decreet was assigned to Robert Mill (or Milne) of Balfarg, the King's master mason, and Patrick Stiell, merchant, burgess of Edinburgh, who were infeft in the same subjects on November 18, 1696. The sasine in their favour narrated that they had built a great new tenement upon the "greater part" of the subjects. The property is referred to in the various documents that passed between Abercrombie, Watson, Mill, and Steill as bounded by Bruce's Close on the west. A property that intervened between Abercrombie's property and Mary King's Close was acquired also by Mill and Steill from Thomas Young of Rosebank, one of the Bailies of Edinburgh. The sasine in their favour bears date November 18th, 1696, and the property is described as bounded on the west by "the lands of the late Robert Scott," and on the east by "the transe of the said [King's] Close." The building erected by Mill and Steill on Scott's property extended also over this property as far as the line of Mary King's Close.

Subsequent sasines of the years 1697, 1698, and 1699 recorded in the protocol books of Æneas MacLeod give the history of the alienation of the different portions of the building erected by Mill and Steill between Bruce's Close and Mary King's Close, and in these documents the name Bruce's Close is replaced by the modern designation, Warriston's Close, as the boundary on the west. A large part of it was acquired in 1699 by the Society

Houses occupied by John Knox

of Writers to the Signet, who ordered a board to be put up with the inscription "Writers' Court," which has been a familiar name ever since. Its boundaries are accurately defined in these and later title-deeds. A sasine of 1702 (Nov. 17) refers to "that new stone tenement of land lately built by Robert Milne, wright, and Patrick Steill, merchant, commonly called The Writers' Court, lying on the north side of the High Street, bounded between the close called Mary King's Close on the east, the close called Warriston's Close on the west. . . ."

The history of the "backlands" of John Broun, father of him who was executed for heresy in 1539, is now complete, along with that of the buildings which had existed on them at different times. They are represented by a strip of land on the eastern side of Warriston's Close, which has been recently appropriated for the extension of the Royal Exchange Buildings, and the corresponding piece on the north of Cockburn Street, between it and the site of the North Loch.

John Knox & Edinburgh

The front portion of the elder John Broun's property, which, it will be remembered, passed into the hands of Mr John Foulis of Colinton, belongs now also to the Corporation of Edinburgh, which thus possesses so much of that long strip of his which extended to the North Loch as is bounded by the High Street on the south and Cockburn Street on the north, and by the line of the present Warriston Close on the west. Mowbray's property, which had John Knox as one of its tenants, contained a house and garden situate, as the better class of houses were situate, at a little distance from the front or high street. John Knox's house was thus either the second or third house in what is now Warriston's Close, and was situated on the east side of the close, with another property—that purchased in 1696 by Mill and Steill from Thomas Young—intervening[1] between it and Mary King's Close,

[1] Reference may be made here to a curious sculptured stone picked up from the foundations of a house in Mary King's Close when the present Cockburn Street was being formed, which is now preserved in the National Museum of Antiquities in Edinburgh. A representation of it is given in Sir Daniel Wilson's "Memorials of Edinburgh," 2nd Edition, II., 20. It represents

Houses occupied by John Knox

which was the next close to the east. The western portion of the Cockburn Hotel now extends over part of the garden that was attached to Mowbray's or Knox's house.

The tenement erected by Mill and Steill stood until quite recently at the north-west corner of the Royal Exchange Square. It was acquired in 1896 by the Corporation of Edinburgh, who demolished it to make way for an extension of the City Chambers buildings. Among the titles of the tenement, which were handed to the city when it was purchased by the Council, is an inventory of writs dated April 8th, 1696, which contains most of the writs in the progress which have been already mentioned. The new additions to the Council Chambers are to occupy its site, and, together with their corridors, will extend right through from the site of Mary King's Close on the east to Warriston's Close on the west. It appears,

in minute detail a death-bed scene, in which "four priests are apparently administering extreme unction to a dying person, presumably of wealth and rank." It is supposed to be fifteenth century work. This stone must have been buried either in or very close to the site of John Knox's garden, if it did not actually form part of his house.

John Knox & Edinburgh

then, that as the building which the Burgh Court and Council Chamber is to replace occupied the "greater part" of the ground on which the house formerly stood that was occupied by John Knox, the western part of the new home for the deliberations of the Town Council of Edinburgh will occupy the exact site of the home for the most important years of his life of the great Scottish Reformer, who was so intimately associated with the Town Council of his day in the years which he spent on this spot.

The next reference to rent paid by the Town Council of Edinburgh is that contained in the minute of November 19th, 1568—the Treasurer ordained "to cause mend and repair the necessaris of Jhone Knox dwelling hous, vpoun the expenssis of Johne Adamsoun and Bessie Otterburn his spous, coniunct fear thairof, and deduce the samyn of thair hous maill, becaus thai haif bene oft tymes requyrit to do the samyn and refussit."

A search has been made in the protocol books of the Town-clerks of Edinburgh for

Houses occupied by John Knox

the purpose of finding the title of John Adamson and Bessie Otterburne his spouse, in the hope of identifying the house in which Knox lived during at least 1568 and 1569. The result leaves no doubt as to the neighbourhood in which Knox resided, but the identification has not proved so exact as that in connection with the properties of Forrester, Ireland, and Mowbray.

It has been found that John Adamson and Bessie Otterburne his spouse were infeft in three different properties, one or other of which must have contained the house referred to in the foregoing minute.

The sasine in favour of John Adamson and Bessie Otterburne in these properties was recorded in the protocol books of Alexander King, Town-clerk, on 31st July 1551. It narrates that Patrick Ireland, Bailie,[1] gave "corporal possession in heritable sasine and conjunct infeftment" to John Adamson, son and heir of Alexander Adamson, burgess of

[1] This is the Patrick Ireland in whose widow's (Margaret Hepburn's) house Knox was residing during part of 1560.

John Knox & Edinburgh

Edinburgh, and to an attorney in name of Elizabeth Otterburne his spouse and the longest liver of them two in (1) All and Whole his, the said John Adamson's lands, built, and waste, under and above, with yard, tail, waste thereof, and their pertinents lying within the wester tenement of Francis Tennand, son and heir of the late Mungo Tennand, Burgess, lying in the burgh of Edinburgh on the north side of the High Street between the easter tenement of the said late Mungo on the east, and the tenement of land of John Symson on the west, and also between the land of Patrick Crighton of Lugton on the south and the North Loch of said burgh on the north; (2) His, the said John Adamson's other land, with halls, chambers, kitchen, pend, and other pertinents lying within the said tenement between the foreland thereof on the south and the said land of the said Patrick Crighton on the north; and (3) His, the said John Adamson's land or mansion under and above with its pertinents lying within the tenement of land

Houses occupied by John Knox

of the heirs of the late John Maxton on the north side of the High Street between a tenement of land of the laird of Haltoun on the east, and a tenement of the late Alexander Bonkill on the west, a land of John Cunyngham on the south, and a land of the Abbot and Convent of Newbottill on the north. These are the only properties which belonged to Adamson and Otterburne, or at least to which they had a duly recorded title.

Further search has been made in the protocol books, and in the inventories of writs and old plans in the possession of the Bank of Scotland, for the purpose of locating these properties, with the following result. The property first described stood partly on what is now a portion of the solum of St Giles Street, and partly on the site of the shop in St Giles Street occupied by Messrs William Green & Sons, law publishers. The property second described lay to the south of the first property, the tenement of Patrick Crighton of Lugton intervening, and was situated immediately behind the front tene-

John Knox & Edinburgh

ment facing the High Street. The third property was situated nearly opposite the corner of High Street and Hunter Square, and lay at some distance north from the High Street. It stood about the south side of the present poultry market.[1]

The progress of titles of each of the three properties subsequent to the sasine above mentioned may be briefly noticed to show how this identification of sites has been reached.

The first infeftment in the first subjects contained in John Adamson's and Bessie Otterburne's sasine after that of John Adamson and Bessie Otterburne themselves was that of Alexander Adamson, their son, who created in 1585 a burden of 100 merks over the property in favour of Hector Rae, merchant.

In 1602 (June 2), a sasine was expede in this portion of the subjects in favour of George Heriot, elder, goldsmith, father of the George Heriot who founded Heriot's Hospital. The description in this sasine varies somewhat from

[1] This market has been removed as these pages are passing through the press (August 1898).

Houses occupied by John Knox

the description given in the sasine of John Adamson and Bessie Otterburne. It is as follows:—" That land or tenement of Alexander Adamson, son and heir of the late John Adamson, lying on the north side of the High Street, opposite the Old Tolbooth, between the lands of the late Gilbert Lauder, on the east, the land of the late Mr Thomas Makcalzeane of Clifton Hall, on the west, the lands of the late Patrick Crighton of Lugton on the south, and the North Loch on the north." The words introduced in this description, "opposite the Old Tolbooth," are of importance, as helping to localise the subjects.

The next sasine found in the Protocol Books is one in 1625 (Jan. 31) in favour of Franciscetta Heriot, spouse of John Ceraris, and lawful daughter of Patrick Heriot, brother-german of the late George Heriot, jeweller to His Majesty, as lawful and nearest heir of the late George Heriot, elder, goldsmith, burgess of Edinburgh, her grandfather. This sasine is in the subjects in which George Heriot, senior, was infeft in 1602, and also in an

John Knox & Edinburgh

annual rent of 100 merks payable out of the subjects. Immediately thereafter the said Franciscetta Heriot, with consent of her spouse, resigned the said subjects and annual rent of 100 merks in favour of the Provost, Bailies, and Council of Edinburgh, who were infeft therein in the person of their Treasurer.

The property thus conveyed to the Provost, Bailies, and Council was held by them for a short time as Governors of Heriot's Hospital, and was sold by them in 1635 (Aug. 18) to Patrick Forbes, merchant, and Elizabeth Newton, his spouse.[1] No information of any importance can be obtained from the various infeftments which followed,[2] until we come to

[1] The Sasine on Vendition and Alienation to Patrick Forbes and Elizabeth Newton bears to have been executed by the Provost, Bailies, and Treasurer of Edinburgh, Mr James Hannay, Dean of St Giles', Mr Alexr. Thomson, and others, ministers of Edinburgh, as Governors of Heriot's Hospital. This Dean Hannay was the only Dean of Edinburgh on the attempted restoration of Episcopacy by Charles I. It was whilst he was reading for the first and last time the prayer-book which had been imposed upon Scotland by Royal command that the tumult occurred in St Giles (1637), in which a stool was hurled at the Dean's head. This was the signal for the disorders that brought about the Civil War and the subsequent beheading of the King.

[2] The following are the remaining links:—1645, April 22d, Sasine to Robert Fynlaw [or Finlay] and Margaret Maisson, his

Houses occupied by John Knox

a sasine of 1691 in favour of Thomas Brown, bookseller, burgess of Edinburgh, which gives the description of the subjects in the terms already mentioned, and adds that a great new stone tenement had lately been built on the subjects by the said Thomas Brown. This stone tenement came into the hands of the Bank of Scotland, who were infeft therein in 1801 (Nov. 12). It was removed when St Giles Street was formed.

The second subjects contained in John Adamson's and Bessie Otterburne's sasine passed in 1585 (Feb. 24) to Alexander Adamson, son and heir of John Adamson and Bessie Otterburne, and from him in 1600 (May 10) to John Aitken, merchant, and then in 1610 (Sep. 22) to Robert Aitken, his son and heir. In Robert Aitken's sasine the description is a little fuller than that given in

spouse; 1654, May 11th, to Sir James Stewart of Kirkfield, Knight, late Provost of Edinburgh; 1666, October 24th, to Alexr. Lessels, merchant, and Margaret Thomson, his spouse; 1686, March 11th, to John Lessels, merchant, burgess of Haddington, brother and heir to the afore-mentioned Alexr. Lessels; 1691, August 15th, to Thomas Brown, bookseller, burgess of Edinburgh, and —— Calderwood, his spouse.

John Knox & Edinburgh

the previous sasines and throws some further light on the locality of the subjects. The description bears that the subjects lay in the close called Adamson's Close, on the east side of the transe thereof, and on the north side of the High Street opposite the Old Tolbooth. Sasines in favour of various parties followed, but as these give no additional information they need not be noticed [1] until we come to a sasine in 1698 (August 24) in favour of Alexander Gavinlock, mason, Burgess of Edinburgh. This Alexander Gavinlock demolished the buildings and erected, partly on the site thereof and partly on the site which intervened between Adamson's property and

[1] The links are as follows:—1631, May 19, John Aitken, son and heir to Robert, who resigned them immediately to James Riddell, merchant, and Margaret Lowrie, his spouse. 1672, March 25, Sasine on resignation by the said John Aitken in favour of the aforesaid late James Riddell, Bailie. 1685, March 18, Decreet of Adjudication at the instance of Andrew Kerr, of the subjects foresaid. 1690, May 7, Letters of Horning thereon, charging the Magistrates of Edinburgh to infeft the said Andrew Kerr. 1697, May 7, "Ane appretiatione by fifteen sworn men by warrand from the Toun Council of Edinburgh, whereby they found that the said Backland acquired by the said Alexander Gavinlock from the said Andrew Kerr on the West side of Bailie Broun's close. . . , they value and estimate at 9 years' purchase, &c."

Houses occupied by John Knox

the High Street, a new stone building which was afterwards known as Gavinlock's Land. The only other sasine remaining to be noticed is that of the Bank of Scotland, which acquired Gavinlock's Land in 1848. The subjects in that sasine are described as the great stone building now called Gavinlock's Land, lying on the north side of the High Street and opposite the head of Forrester's Wynd.

The situation of these two properties of John Adamson and Bessie Otterburne is thus placed beyond doubt. They both lay "opposite the Old Tolbooth." They were on the north side of the High Street, "opposite the head of Forrester's Wynd." A tenement intervened between the second of them and the High Street, and this second property was in its turn separated from the one first named by the lands of Patrick Crichton of Lugton. The second property was reached by a close which is called Adamson's Close in the sasines of 1610 and 1631. The buildings on the east side of the present St Giles Street cover

John Knox & Edinburgh

the site of the old "Adamson's Close,"[1] and the pavement on the east side of the street is formed over part of the properties that belonged in the sixteenth century to John Adamson and Elizabeth Otterburne, the landlords of Knox, the Reformer.

The third subjects contained in John Adamson's and Bessie Otterburne's sasine passed in 1585, on the death of John Adamson, to Alexander Adamson, his son, and after various infeftments,[2] which all give the same description as that given in Adamson's sasine, they came in 1684 into the hands of Robert Newlands, glover, Burgess of Edinburgh. Robert Newlands, son of this Robert New-

---

[1] The Close giving access to properties here was known from the owners at different times as Adamson's Close, Heriot's Close, and Broun's Close. See Sasine of 1600, May 10, 1610, September 22, and 1631, May 19, for "Adamson's Close"; the "Appretiatione" of May 7, 1697, for "Bailie Broun's Close"; the Sasine of August 24, 1698, referred to above for "Hartis" (sic) or "Heriot's Close."

[2] 1602, January 15, George Kirkwood, Albany Herald. 1613, October 23, George Kirkwood, younger son of preceding. 1647, April 9, Elizabeth Kirkwood, daughter of preceding. 1675, September 13, Sir James Standsfield of Newmilns, Knight. 1684, August 18, Robert Newlands, glover.

Houses occupied by John Knox

lands of 1684, appears to have erected a new tenement on the subjects. A sasine is found, of date June 22d, 1711, proceeding on an obligation by him in which the subjects are described as "the said Robert Newlands' tenement on the north side of the High Street, in the close called the Mid Fleshmarket Close, on the east side of the transe thereof, between the land sometime of Alexander Borthwick, vintner, on the east, the tenement of the late Robert Hepburne of Whitburgh on the north, a tenement of Robert Brown, bookseller, on the south, and the said close on the west." It will be seen that this new description does not contain anything to identify it with the old description contained in John Adamson's sasine. There is no doubt, however, that the two descriptions relate to the same property. Both point to the same spot. A sasine of January 21st, 1691, mentions that John Maxton's tenement, referred to in the description in Adamson's sasine, lay "on the north side of the High Street opposite the Salt Tron," thus establishing the fact that the locality of the old description was the same as that of the new.[1]

The subjects known as Newlands' Land passed through various hands after Newlands ceased to be connected with it, and ultimately, on 15th January 1790, a sasine is found in favour of the city of Edinburgh of the ground storey of the tenement.[2] That sasine gives some further information in regard to the locality of the subjects. It mentions that they lay on the west side of Bull's Close,

---

[1] Other evidence from the Stent Rolls, the Register of Deeds, the Dean of Guild Court Records, and the titles of the adjoining properties, which it is not necessary to go into minutely, can be adduced to confirm this.

[2] Extract from "Titles to the Edinburgh Markets":—"1771, September 6, Disposition by William Wilson of Soonhope, writer in Edinburgh, trustee for Robert Bailie, merchant in Edinburgh, conform to the said Robert Bailie's trust disposition, dated 12th March 1756, and registered in the Books of Council and Session, 22 August 1789, in favour of the said Wm. Wilson and other creditors, of the ground storey of Newlands' Land, lying on the north side of the High Street, on the west side of Bull's Close, as bounded in the ancient rights and infeftments thereof, in favour of John Stewart, writer in Edinburgh, who has right to the same by assignation from William Reid, merchant, of date 6 Sept. 1771, who bought the same at a roup on 9 Augt. 1771; and which ground storey of Newlands' Land was disponed by Thomas Scott, Clerk to the Signet, Commissioner of Thomas Balleny, tenant in South Parks of Lesly, to the City of Edinburgh, on 15 January 1790."

Houses occupied by John Knox

that being the close immediately to the east of the Mid Fleshmarket Close. The sasine of 1711, taken along with this, suggests that the tenement extended between the two closes. It would appear that the property thus acquired by the city now forms part of the Flesh and Poultry Markets.[1] It may be added that Bull's Close and Mid Fleshmarket Close are not now in existence. They were swept away when Cockburn Street was formed.

Bull's Close was called at an earlier period Adamson's Close, or the Caichepeele Close. It is thus designated in the Stent Book of the City of Edinburgh, 1634-36, "Adamson's, or the Caichepeele Close, right north of the Salt Tronne." It was referred to also as "Ketch Peil or Fleshmarket Close" in a disposition of so recent a date as 1856. A catchpool or caichepeele was a tennis court,[2]

---

[1] See note, page 92.

[2] The following extract from the Town Treasurer's Accounts refers to this popular game of the time:—"The expenses maid upone the marriage of the Quenis Grace, with the Convoy the [blank] day of Julij Anno 1558. [Here follows five pages of detailed accounts. One item is,] Item for twa dosoun of cachepull

John Knox & Edinburgh

and the word suggests another item of identification between John Adamson's and Newlands' properties. John Adamson's property is described as bounded by a land of the Abbot and Convent of Newbottill (or Newbattle) on the north, and this description is a permanent one until 1711, when it and the other boundaries are replaced by what seem to be the descriptions of the owners of the adjoining properties at that date. The former description occurs in the sasine of August 18th, 1684, conveying John Adamson's property from Sir James Standsfield of Newmilns to Robert Newlands, although the abbots and monastery of Newbattle had long been things of the past. This Newbattle property passed in 1549 (February 12) by sasine on a charter of feuferme to a James Adamson, and it is stated that the charter was granted because the said James Adamson gave large sums of money to the abbot to rebuild the tenement, which had been cast

balls cled with gold fuilze [leaf gold] till being hing upone the tree upone the Trone, price viij^d."

Houses occupied by John Knox

down "when our old enemies of England burnt the town of Edinburgh." It had naturally the same boundaries in part as the property owned by John Adamson and transferred to himself and Elizabeth Otterbourne in 1551, which it touched on the south, these being the strip of ground owned by the Laird of Haltoun on the east and that owned by Marion Bonkill on the west. In a sasine of resignation of 100 marks yearly out of the property in 1566, it is described as "a tenement of the said James Adamson, with yard, catchepool, and waste land adjacent thereto, on the north side of the High Street, between the lands of the heirs of the Laird of Haltoun on the east, the lands of Marion Bonkle on the west, and the lands of John Adamson, son and heir of the late Alexander Adamson, on the south, and the North Loch on the North." Newlands' property was in Bull's Close, which was opposite the Salt Tron.[1] The Tron itself has been removed

[1] A "Tron" was a weighing machine. The "Salt Tron" was the machine used for weighing salt. It stood in the High Street, almost opposite the west end of the present Tron Church.

John Knox & Edinburgh

long since, but its name is still perpetuated in the "Tron Church."

Adamson's or the Caichepeele Close was opposite the Salt Tron, and is identified doubly through the Catchpool referred to in James Adamson's sasine of 1566. All were on the north side of the High Street, and all the items converge, as has been shown, on the second property from the High Street on the opposite side to the corner of the High Street and the present Hunter Square. This property of John Adamson and Bessie Otterburne and James Adamson's property—that which was formerly possessed by the Abbot of Newbattle—with the exception of a part of John Adamson's property that was thrown into the roadway of Cockburn Street, have been acquired recently by the proprietors of *The Scotsman*. New buildings are to be erected on their sites.

Knox must have lived during 1568 and 1569, if not longer, in one of these three houses thus accurately identified—the second property from the High Street on the east side of the

Houses occupied by John Knox

present St Giles Street, or the fourth property from the High Street in the same quarter, or the second from the High Street opposite the corner of the present Hunter Square, but no indication has been discovered so far which identifies a particular one of the three as his. That must still be left uncertain. There are nothing but probabilities to work upon. But the probabilities of the case would seem to point to the house referred to as second in the sasine of 1551. The third house—that opposite the Salt Tron—was scarcely conveniently enough situated, from all that is known concerning the residences of Knox, to serve as a manse for the minister of St Giles'. The old manses had been in the churchyard, and the Magistrates seem to have endeavoured always to provide a "lodging" for Knox from which the church should be equally easy of access. This third house stood about forty yards from the High Street, and the Salt Tron was about a hundred and ninety yards from the present north entrance of the church. Either of the other two houses would have

John Knox & Edinburgh

been more readily chosen for the purpose. They were both within a stone's throw of the church, right opposite the site of the present Buccleuch statue. Either was equally convenient. The second was possibly a little more so. It was, besides, from all the descriptions, the better house of the two. It had "halls, chambers, kitchen, pend, and other pertinents," every convenience, as would be advertised now, for a gentleman's family. There is no mention of a hall in the first house. The Town Council treated Knox not merely as a gentleman, but as a nobleman, and his house would be one of the best.[1] They had built a study for him above the hall of Mowbray's house and they were almost certain to choose as good a house for him when he returned to Edinburgh after his temporary exile.

No trace has been found of any reference which could imply that Knox had changed his

---

[1] "His stipend was considerably higher than the salary of the judges of the Court of Session, and not much lower than that of the English judges of the same period." "St Giles', Edinburgh," by J. Cameron Lees, D.D., LL.D., &c., p. 141.

Houses occupied by John Knox

residence between November 23, 1569, when rent was paid to John Adamson, and May 1571, when Knox was forced to leave Edinburgh for a time. He returned from St Andrews in August 1572, and the assumption that he re-occupied the house he had left in 1571 is as reasonable as any other in the absence of any definite proof. By a curious coincidence, which may not be without bearing on the question, a John Adamson's name—"Jhone Adamesoun"—appears as the first of three witnesses to his will, which was executed at St Andrews in May 1572. John Adamson, his Edinburgh landlord, was also one of his elders, and it is more than probable that he was amongst the number of those opposed to the Queen's party who were forced to leave Edinburgh along with Knox in obedience to the proclamation of Kirkcaldy of Grange. If that was so, both Adamson and Knox, as well as the others who had been compelled to leave, would naturally take up their abode on their return in the houses which they had left.

John Knox & Edinburgh

It is not without interest to notice the class of house and the character of the neighbourhood in which Knox was always lodged. The houses selected for his residence were amongst the best in the burgh. Forrester's house had been already chosen for the residence of an English Ambassador, and had been occupied by Lord Seton immediately before its occupation by Knox. This Lord Seton was one of the most prominent of the Scottish nobles, and was at the time Lord Provost of Edinburgh, though his duties were discharged by deputy. Patrick Ireland's house was itself a building of some consequence, and between it and John Adamson's "first house" lay the house of Mr Thomas Makcalzeane, or M'Calzean, a notable citizen of Edinburgh, who was President of the Town Council under Seton, and became afterwards Lord Provost.[1] The house of Adam Bothwell, Bishop of Orkney, who performed the marriage ceremony between Queen Mary and Bothwell in 1567,

---

[1] Makcalzeane (M'Calzean, M'Callione) was also one of the "elders" of Edinburgh. Bannatyne's "Transactions," p. 333.

Houses occupied by John Knox

was in the immediate vicinity, with Byer's Close intervening.

Warriston's Close—which was the name afterwards given to that lane on the north side of the High Street in which Mowbray's house was situated—has a long and interesting history through its occupants at various times. It was known successively as Bruce's Close, Craig's Close, and Warriston's Close, and each name pointed to a well-known family as residing in one of the houses to which the close afforded an entrance from the High Street. The Bruce referred to in the earliest name by which the Close is designated is Bruce of Binning, in Stirlingshire. These Bruces were cadets of the family of Bruce of Stonehouse and Airth, which was already a distinguished family in the reign of James III. Their property was on the west side of the Close, on the opposite side from Mowbray's property on the east, but a little further south. The mansion to the north of Bruce's "lodging" was owned in Knox's time by a family named Craig, and was occupied by its most notable representative, "Sir Thomas Craig," as he was styled by order of James VI., after he had repeatedly declined the honour of knighthood. "He was succeeded in the old mansion by his son, Sir Lewis Craig, and had the satisfaction of pleading as advocate while Sir Lewis presided on the Bench under the title of Lord Wrightslands. The house was subsequently occupied by Sir George Urquhart of Cromarty, and still later by Sir Robert Baird of Saughton Hall, before it passed to the more celebrated residenter from whom the latest designation of this ancient alley is derived. The eminent statesman, Sir Archibald Johnston of Warriston, nephew of its older inhabitant Sir Thomas Craig, appears from the titles to have purchased from his cousin, Sir Lewis Craig, the house adjoining his own, on the west side of the Close, immediately below the one last described."[1] This Johnston of Warriston was prominent in the opposition given to the schemes of Charles I. He assumed the title of Lord Warriston on his promotion to the

[1] Sir Daniel Wilson's "Memorials of Edinburgh," Vol II., 15-16.

Houses occupied by John Knox

Bench. After the Restoration he fled to France, but was given up by the French King, and brought back to Edinburgh, where he was executed with peculiar marks of indignity at the Market Cross.

It was to Mowbray's house on the east side of this close, which overlooked the gardens of these mansions, that Knox brought his second wife, and it was here that he entertained the English Ambassador and the Duke of Chatelherault. After Knox left it for John Adamson's house, Mowbray's house was let to the Archbishop of Glasgow, and two years afterwards it was occupied by John Belsches, a prominent advocate of the period. In a later generation, James Murray, Lord Philiphaugh, one of the Judges appointed after the Revolution, occupied part of the front land, above the entrance to Warriston's Close. Later still, in the borderland of fact and fancy, and on the very site of Knox's house, Writers' Court was the home of Clerihugh's, or the "Star and Garter" tavern, associated inseparably with the "high jinks" of Coun-

John Knox & Edinburgh

sellor Pleydell and his associates, as described in "Guy Mannering" by Sir Walter Scott.[1]

[1] "Clerihugh's tavern was of old the favourite resort of our civic dignitaries for those 'douce festivities' that were then deemed indispensable to the satisfactory settlement of all city affairs. The wags of last century used to tell of a certain city treasurer who, on being applied to for a new rope for the Tron Kirk bell, summoned the Council to deliberate on the demand; an adjournment to Clerihugh's Tavern, it was hoped, might facilitate the settlement of so weighty a matter, but one dinner proved insufficient, and it was not till their third banquet that the application was referred to a committee, who spliced the old bell rope and settled the bill!" Sir Daniel Wilson's "Memorials of Edinburgh," Vol II., 17.

The Legend of "John Knox's House"

The Legend of "John Knox's House"

A HOUSE at the Netherbow in Edinburgh is popularly called "John Knox's House," and is said to have got the name from having been the residence of Knox, the Reformer. There has not been discovered a shadow of historical proof for this statement, and the tradition that Knox lived in it can be traced back only for ninety-two years from this present date of eighteen hundred and ninety-eight. This leaves a gap of 234 years between the death of the Knox of Queen Mary's time and the first trace that any such belief existed.

Once the legend was started that John Knox had resided in a house at the Netherbow it grew apace. In its first two appearances in public it was singularly plain and

John Knox & Edinburgh

unadorned, but these are faults that were amply atoned for before long. Stark, in his "Picture of Edinburgh,"[1] which was published in 1806, describes the supposed house as follows:—"Among the antiquities of Edinburgh may be mentioned the house of the great Scottish Reformer, John Knox. It stands on the north side, at the foot of the High Street, and, projecting into the street, reduces it nearly one-half of its width." It has been stated that "the value of tradition is a question of circumstances,"[2] but the "circumstances" here is a bald assertion with no possible suggestion of proof.

It would seem indeed as if at the very outset there had been some little doubt as to which particular house in that neighbourhood should be associated with Knox. A Dean of Guild process of the year 1839 assigns the name to the house immediately east of that now known as John Knox's house.

---

[1] See page 167.

[2] C. J. Guthrie, in "Proceedings of Society of Antiquaries, Scotland," 1891, p. 334, "Is John Knox's House entitled to the name?"

"John Knox's House"

This house is spoken of elsewhere as Lord Balmerino's house,[1] and the process states that "on the morning of Sabbath, the 17th February 1839, that old wooden tenement (commonly called John Knox's Land) on the north side of the Netherbow, Edinburgh, belonging to Matthew Frier, baker, St Patrick's Square, fell down into the street, and that parts of it still remain in a tottering condition." Warrant was granted on the 21st ordering that the remaining parts of this tenement should be taken down or made secure. But the name "John Knox's Land" was not attached to Frier's tenement alone. The Dean of Guild officer reported on February 18th that another house, referred to also as "commonly called John Knox's Land," and apparently the present "John Knox's House," was "in an insufficient and dangerous state to the inhabitants thereof and the public." The fall of Frier's tenement had left those on each side of it insecure. This second "John Knox's Land" was the

[1] See Sir Daniel Wilson's "Memorials of Edinburgh," II., 53.

John Knox & Edinburgh

tenement on the west. If it was not so situated, the expression "John Knox's *Land*" of these documents of 1839 cannot be connected with the "John Knox's *House*" of to-day.

It will be noticed that the description given by Stark, bald as it is, is much more definite than that given in the Dean of Guild Court proceedings of 1839. It connects Knox with one particular house, and apparently with that known now as John Knox's House. Taking that for granted, a search which has been made in the Dean of Guild Court Records has pushed the modern history of the house fifteen years farther back than the date of the publication of Stark's volume. These documents show that the upper storeys or flats of this tenement had become ruinous by 1791, and the building was before the Dean of Guild Court regularly between that date and 1852, when it was reported at last to be "now perfectly safe both in respect to the inhabitants and public." Warrant was granted on August 28th, 1791, by the Court

"John Knox's House"

at the suit of one of the proprietors that the roof should be repaired as the rain was finding its way through the third and fourth storeys into the second; and a process was issued on July 19th, 1798, against the proprietor of the upper storey for his share of the expense; but in neither of these official papers is there any suggestion of any association with the name of Knox.

We arrive on surer ground a few years later. A petition to the Magistrates by the Procurator-Fiscal, of date December 30th, 1847, complained that the fourth storey of a tenement of land, commonly called "John Knox's Land," or "Knox's Land," had "for a period of more than three years lain waste and uninhabited," and craved authority to deal with it in accordance with the Act of Charles II.,—"Anent Ruinous Houses in Royal Burghs." Comparison of the proprietors' names in 1791, 1798, and 1847 shows that this building which was "commonly called John Knox's Land" in 1847, and reported to be "waste and uninhabited" in

John Knox & Edinburgh

the fourth storey, is the same building which was reported to have a defective roof in the former of these years, but which had been repaired by 1798. After 1847 there is no doubt that the expression "John Knox's Land," or "John Knox's House," means the house at the Netherbow, which, after many vicissitudes, came into possession of the Free Church in 1868, and is still shown as the house in which the Reformer lived. Two of the surnames of the owners given in the Process of July 19th, 1798, appear again in the documents relative to the second-named "John Knox's Land" of 1839, and authorise the supposition that they also refer to this same house.

The next writer after Stark who mentions Knox as having resided in the neighbourhood of the Netherbow is M'Crie, whose "Life of Knox" appeared originally in 1811. His statement is not much more explicit than that of Stark. It is given in a footnote, as if it probably were considered of not sufficient importance or authenticity for the text:—"The

"John Knox's House"

house which the Reformer possessed is situated near the bottom of the High Street, a little below the Fountain Well. These three words are inscribed on the wall: "ΘΕΟΣ, DEUS, GOD."[1] This occurs in a reference to Smeton as the authority for the last public appearance of Knox, after having presided and preached in St Giles at the installation of Lawson as his colleague and successor. The exact words that Smeton used are as follows:—"After he had blessed the people, with his wonted cheerful spirit, but with feeble body, and leaning on his staff, he departed to his house accompanied by almost the whole meeting, from which he did not afterwards come forth alive"[2] It will be noticed that Smeton gives no indication whatever in these words of where John Knox was residing; and the natural inference would be, that, in the feeble state of health in which Knox was at this time, it could not be so far from St Giles as the Netherbow, if he was to

---

[1] "Life of John Knox," Edition 1855, p. 270.

[2] "Eximii viri Joannis Knoxii . . . Vera . . . Historia," by Thomas Smeton, Principal of the University of Glasgow, 1579.

walk there even with assistance. But of this more later.

After 1811 the legend becomes embellished and it assumes a variety of forms. It was distinctly ornate by 1823. Sir Daniel Wilson quoted in the "Proceedings of the Society of Antiquaries for 1890-91," pp. 157-8, the following description of the house as given by Robert Chambers in his "Traditions of Edinburgh," the first edition of which appeared in the year given above:—"Close beneath the window there has long existed a curious effigy of the Reformer stuck upon the corner, and apparently holding forth to the passers-by. Of this no features were for a long time discernible till Mr Dryden (then tenant of the house) took shame to himself for the neglect it was experiencing and got it daubed over in glaring oil colours, at his own expense. Thus a red nose and two intensely black eyes were brought strongly out on the mass of face, and a pair of white iron Geneva bands, with a new black gown, completed the resuscitation." These sentences do not appear in the

"John Knox's House"

revised reprint of 1868, but many other items confirmatory of the tradition are given. John Knox's study was there, that the magistrates ordered for him in October 1561; the window was there, from which he harangued the crowd below; there was a small room still to be seen, which served as a baptistery; and there was a well, as the house in which Knox lived was known to have a well. And the window where his effigy appeared was the window through which a musket-ball was fired at the Reformer's head before he left Edinburgh in 1571.

A new edition, the seventh, of M'Crie's "Life" appeared in 1855, edited with notes by his son. The legend appears in one of these notes much in the same form as in Chambers, but with important differences. Knox took up his abode in the house at the Netherbow in 1560, and it remained his principal residence until his death in 1572. It was whilst living here that he lost his first wife, and it was to this house that he brought his second. It was through one of its windows

John Knox & Edinburgh

that a musket-shot was discharged which must infallibly have killed him if he had been occupying his usual seat. It was here that he penned his "History." It was to this house that he "crept down the street" never to leave it alive, and his study, "undoubtedly" the one ordered in 1561, remained very much in its original form.

Every one of the statements made by Chambers and the editor of M'Crie's "Life" has been proved, where proof of any kind is possible, to be incorrect. It was shown before the publication of the 1855 edition of M'Crie that the figure on the outside of the house was not Knox at all but Moses, though the statement that it was the Reformer preaching in a pulpit was repeated by Chambers in 1868. The editor of M'Crie's "Life" mentions the correction of the legend, and it is not unimportant to observe that M'Crie himself seems not to have known, in 1811, that the figure was intended for either Moses or Knox.[1] He

[1] It is also important to notice that Stark, in 1806, could say nothing to associate this figure with either the house or Knox. "Whether the figure is meant to represent the reformer himself,

"John Knox's House"

quotes the inscription correctly to which Moses is pointing, but says nothing further about it. The pulpit was an altogether modern affair, copied from the pulpit of St George's Church, which was erected in 1814. The red nose and the Geneva bands and black gown disappear with Knox himself. The "Study" was not the study ordered in 1561. Knox did not live here from 1560 to 1572. He is not known to have preached from any window. It is not known why he should have kept a private baptistery. There was no well in this house when it was examined in 1896. So much for the embellishments. The legend is left now in the form in which it was known to Stark and M'Crie—the simple assertion that Knox lived in Edinburgh at a house then and still existent in the Netherbow.

The legend also differs considerably and vitally in the mouth of its different narrators respecting the period of Knox's occupation of

or not, is not known; but whoever it is, he seems to have been hardly used, part of the stone on which it is executed being broken off either by accident or design."—"Picture of Edinburgh," p. 103.

John Knox & Edinburgh

"John Knox's House." Stark and M'Crie say nothing definite. M'Crie's editor says he resided here generally from 1560 to 1572, the whole period of his settled career in Edinburgh. Chambers says the tradition was that this was the residence or manse of John Knox during his incumbency as minister of Edinburgh, from 1560 until (with few interruptions) his death in 1572. This is an integral part of the full-blown legend, and the statement passed unchallenged until 1891, when it was shown for the first time from the original Council records, in a paper contributed to the Society of Antiquaries, that Knox lived elsewhere between 1560 and 1569.[1]

Sir Daniel Wilson, who, as secretary to the Society of Antiquaries, had done good service in securing the preservation of the old house in 1849, though in the mistaken idea that it was John Knox's manse, attempted in 1891 a mild justification of the tradition is so far as that there was nothing inconsistent with

[1] "Proceedings of the Society of Antiquaries of Scotland, 1891," page 138: "John Knox and his manse," by Peter Miller, F.S.A. Scot."

"John Knox's House"

probability in the belief that the house was Knox's latest home,[1] but he acknowledged immediately afterwards that there was "no evading the fact that Knox never did live in 'John Knox's House.'"[2] A reply was attempted in another paper read before the Society of Antiquaries,[3] in which Sir Daniel Wilson was quoted as one of the "most competent antiquaries" who "have admitted the justice of the claim." The writer of this paper maintained boldly that "every circumstance accords with the truth of the tradition."[4] "After doing their very worst, they leave three years and ten months up to 24th November 1572, when Knox died, during which they are unable to address any proof whatever against the tradition that he resided in the house in question. I challenge their conclusions as to the preceding period."[5]

[1] "Proceedings of the S.A.Scot., 1891," p. 156.

[2] "Private Letters of Sir Daniel Wilson, Edinburgh," printed for private circulation, 1897, letter dated "11th January 1891."

[3] "Proceedings of the S.A.Scot., 1891," p. 335: "Is 'John Knox's House' Entitled to the Name!" by Charles J. Guthrie, advocate, F.S.A.Scot.

[4] "Proceedings of the S.A.Scot., 1891," p. 336.

[5] "Proceedings of the S.A.Scot., 1891," p. 337.

John Knox & Edinburgh

Definite proof was furnished by the original writer in another communication to the Society of Antiquaries, of date May 8th, 1893,[1] that Knox lived in other houses from 1560-1569, though the sites of the houses were incorrectly given; but the champion of the legend was not dismayed. He returned to the charge in an article in the "Free Church Monthly" for September 1896. The admission is made there that Knox "certainly occupied other houses in Edinburgh," though it is qualified by the introductory words, "whether his residence in this house was limited to his later years or not"; but all the old irrelevant statements are repeated concerning the "public interest centring in Knox's last days round that house," and the article closes with the emphatic assertion, "It is enough for us that Knox died there."

When Sir Daniel Wilson published the second edition of his "Memorials of Edinburgh" in 1891, though he had the strongest desire to adhere as far as possible to the

[1] "Proceedings of the S.A.Scot., 1893," p. 406.

"John Knox's House"

popular belief, he could only make the colourless assertion that " in the absence of other evidence we may welcome such guidance as tradition supplies, and still think of the house that has so long borne his name as the lodging where his last days were spent."[1] Against this must be set his private opinion quoted above. The latest biographer of Knox, P. Hume Brown, in his "Life of John Knox," published in 1895, could not go further than Sir Daniel Wilson in the "Memorials" of 1891. "To Mosman's house ['John Knox's House ']," Hume Brown says, "at all events, tradition points as the residence; and if we attach any weight to the tradition, that house would in all probability be the one in which his last days were spent. . . . Against the tradition that points to Mosman's house as a residence of Knox no satisfactory evidence has been adducd."[2]

The legend has thus dwindled away to the original tradition that Knox lived some time or other in "John Knox's House," and that

[1] Vol. II., p. 50.   [2] Vol. II., pp. 318, 319.

John Knox & Edinburgh

the tradition ought to be received because there is no satisfactory proof that he did not live in it. By the same method of argument, one might be called upon to prove that Knox did not live in any particular old house in Edinburgh in which a few persons might be pleased to state he lived. The onus is rather the other way. A story was started about the beginning of the century—it would seem on no evidence whatever—that Knox lived in this house at the Netherbow; the world has been looking for some proof since that he did live in it; but no proof is vouchsafed except that people generally have come to call it " John Knox's House."

It has been proved already by the extracts given in the chapter of this book dealing with the residences of John Knox in Edinburgh that he lived in other houses between 1560 and November 23, 1569. Documentary proof fails us between this date and his death in November 1572, for the simple reason that no documentary proof of the kind already quoted is known to exist. It was a very

"John Knox's House"

troublous period in Edinburgh—a time of practically civil war. The Treasurer's accounts show a blank from 1567 down to 1581, and there are no records of the meetings of the Town Council from 1571 to 1573. The only period as to which almost nothing can be said is that between November 1569 and May 1571, when Knox was constrained by his friends to leave Edinburgh. This interval of eighteen months is of no special importance in dealing with the picturesque aspects of the legend, as it was not during it that the affecting scene occurred when Knox was conveyed to his home after his last sermon, nor could anything that occurred during those months have consecrated his residence as the Mecca of Scottish religionism and the spot hallowed by his death. As it is, we know that in November 1569 he was living in a very different quarter of Edinburgh, and there is not a hint anywhere that he changed his residence at that time. Moreover, as will be shown hereafter, the history of the house at the Netherbow is well known for the

John Knox & Edinburgh

years covered by Knox's ministry in Edinburgh; and it was about the most unlikely house in the burgh that would have been chosen by him or for his use.

There is left still for examination the period of less than three months which elapsed between the return of Knox to Edinburgh in August 1572 and his death on November 24th. Routed out of the earlier years, the legend takes refuge here. The same remarks apply to these months which have already been made concerning the eighteen months that followed November 1569, with this additional note, that since it has been shown that there is not the faintest shadow of reason for believing in the original form of the statement so far as that Knox is said to have lived at a particular house in the Netherbow for the eleven years from 1560 to 1571, there is no reason whatever for assuming that the statement is true concerning this particular twelve weeks. There is, firstly, no possible proof. There are, in the second place, no Council documents. In the third place, the

"John Knox's House"

history and ownership of the Netherbow house are well known, and everything points to its occupation by the owner himself. In the fourth place, the authorities for the period make not the slightest allusion to the Netherbow. And fifthly, the condition of Knox's health made his residence at the Netherbow, under the circumstances narrated by these authorities, practically impossible.

Dealing with these items seriatim, there is, firstly, no possible proof. There is nothing but the assertion; feeble and unpretending, as given by Stark and M'Crie, that a house at the Netherbow was the Reformer's; amplified by their successors; and paraded more recently in a Free Church mantle to hallow the walls at the Netherbow as, if not sanctified by Knox through life, his at least by his death. There are, secondly, no Council documents. None affecting this period are known to exist. It was suggested, in what seemed a serious communication to the Society of Antiquaries in 1891,[1] that the

[1] "Proceedings of S.A. Scot., 1891," p. 338.

absence of any entries of payments of rent after 1569 was due to the fact that Knox "evidently paid his own house rent" during these years.[1] This is hardly worth referring to, except as a sample of the arguments used to bolster up the legend. The pithy remark was once made that "it is evident" means "we cannot prove," and no proof of the assertion concerning payment of rent by Knox has even been suggested. The truth is, as has been stated before, that the records for this period are very defective. In the

---

[1] "Second, it is alleged that the house belonged in Knox's time to James Mosman, the goldsmith, and that the Town Council Records contain no entries of payment of rent to James Mosman. Neither they do; they do not contain payment of rent after 1569 to James Mosman or to anybody else, for the very good reason that, as the Council Records show, Knox was getting in these later years a regular stipend, out of which he evidently paid his own house rent." It is difficult to criticise this statement. The Council Records do not show that Knox was getting a regular stipend "in these later years," which must mean, if words mean anything, those after 1569. The last reference to payment of stipend "to John Knox" is that under date June 19, 1562. Several references are made to the subject of the support of the "ministrie" in 1570 (August 11, August 24, October 25, November 1, November 15), and they all imply that difficulty was being experienced in obtaining the sums required, but John Knox's name is not mentioned. (See also page 41.) John Knox seems to have been in the receipt of a regular stipend (M'Crie's

"John Knox's House"

third place, a good deal is known about the Netherbow house—it is fairly prominent in legal documents of its time, and its owner is well known—but there is no reference anywhere to any possible connection with Knox. When we say "the Netherbow house," we should say rather "the house that formerly stood at the Netherbow," of which the present house is to a large extent a reproduction, for very little of the present structure can claim an antiquity of fifty years.

Nothing of the history of the Netherbow house was known when the legend was origi-

"Life," 1855, p. 406), but the Council Records do not say so, further than that he received a regular quarterly allowance during 1560, which was continued for 1561. The entries referring to stipend afterwards imply, that a change had been made in the method of obtaining the sums required, and that the amount to be depended on by the ministers was by no means certain. (See page 35.) The stipend referred to by M'Crie was not paid by the burgh of Edinburgh. The last entries of house rent paid for Knox are those of March 4, 1568-9, and November 23, 1569. The real reason why these entries stop is noted in the text. The whole paper, however, is well worth reading as a specimen of legal ingenuity bolstering up a bad cause. It contains the substance of the later article in the "Free Church Monthly" for September 1896, and of the statements made concerning Knox in the excellent handbook to the so-called "John Knox's House" ("John Knox and John Knox's House") by the same author.

nated, and when this history was accidentally discovered written upon the walls of the house itself, the legend had got a forty years' start. Light was thrown upon the past for the first time when during the repairs made after its demolition had been ordered by the Dean of Guild in 1849 some dilapidated wooden excrescences were removed which had been added by its later owners or occupants. The so-called "preaching window" disappeared, and a fine renaissance window and sculptured tablet were disclosed. The tablet bore a shield charged with three crowns on a chevron between three oak trees, with the initials I. M. and M. A. on either side. These letters and arms afforded the clue. Reference was made to Stodart's "Scottish Arms," the register of the Great Seal, and the protocol books of the city of Edinburgh, and the story of the house revealed itself beyond doubt.

A building which existed on this site in 1525 had belonged to John Arres and Christina Reidpeth, his wife. This had, no doubt, dis-

"John Knox's House"

appeared with the others when Edinburgh was burnt by Hertford in 1544. But in 1556 another house on the same site belongs to James Mosman and Mariot Arres, and the property remains in the possession of this James Mosman, with one significant short interval, until the forfeiture of his property after Mosman's execution in 1573 as an adherent of Queen Mary. The arms are the arms of Mosman as given by Nisbet and Stodart, with the addition of three crowns on the chevron, to indicate that the bearer was a goldsmith like his father, who made the closed arches that still adorn the Scottish Crown. The initials are those of James Mosman and his wife, through whom he came into possession of the property. In 1568, James Mosman and Mariot Arres conveyed this house to John Mosman, goldsmith, their son and his heirs in fee, but reserved to themselves the liferent for their whole lives. We learn from a sasine of February 23d, 1571, that Mariot Arres was dead, and that James Mosman was about to marry for the second time. So what

John Knox & Edinburgh

was more natural than that he should secure a residence for his wife in what was probably then one of the best houses in Edinburgh. He bought back the fee from his son, and immediately infeft himself and his future spouse Janet King in the family residence in the Netherbow. Where does Knox come in? Nowhere. It was quite a common practice to insert the name of the occupying tenant in the conveyance of any property disposed of, and in at least two cases John Knox's name is so mentioned in connection with one of the houses in which he undoubtedly lived, but there is no mention of him here.[1] The names of

---

[1] The following are samples of recent statements made on behalf of the legend:—"First, it is said that the titles of the house made no mention of Knox. This is the suggestion of a layman, which, to any one skilled in title-deeds, will only provoke a smile. You look in titles for the names of proprietors, not tenants: and I know neither evidence nor probability that Knox owned any part of the house in question."—C. J. Guthrie in "Proceedings of S.A.Scot., 1891," p. 338. "Neither in any writing of Knox nor in any contemporary writing about Knox is there a description of his Edinburgh residence to enable us to localise it. He never owned a house in Edinburgh, therefore title-deeds give no clue."—C. J. Guthrie in "Free Church Monthly," September 1896, p. 208. The recklessness of these assertions will become manifest when contrasted with facts. A glance over some extracts taken from the titles of the houses

"John Knox's House"

owners remain unchanged in the successive title-deeds often for centuries, and where the property has had a well-known tenant, his name is introduced by way of identification long after he had ceased to reside in it, and

dealt with in this investigation reveals the following names of occupying tenants, which had been introduced to identify the properties when these were not occupied by the owners:—
1. Mosman's House, which is the one referred to in the above-quoted extracts:—Edinburgh Protocols, Alexander Guthrie, Vol. XII., fol. 149, 22 May 1600, Occupying tenants' names, Murdoch Brown, James Maistertoun. Do. Do., fol. 150, Murdoch Brown, Andrew Smyth. Alex. Strachan's Protocol, Vol. I., fol. 26, 22 Dec. 1699, "Lately possessed by the said David Murray," "sometime possessed by the late Murdoch Brown," "the late James Masterton," "thereafter by the relict of John Mein and Mrs Robert Smith, then her spouse;" "sometime possessed by Andrew Smith, shoemaker;" the late John Baxter. 2. Mowbray's House—Alex. Guthrie's Protocol Books, Vol. III., fol. 41, 8 April 1563, John Knox, minister. Register of Deeds, Vol. 8, fol. 1, 24 March 1564, "Johnne Knox, minister of Edinburgh." Do. Vol. III., fol. 40, 29 April 1630, John Belches, advocate. Sir William Thomson's Protocol Books, II., 239, 13 Oct. 1652, "sometime occupied by John Belsches, advocate." J. Rocheid's Protocol Books, II., 411, 22 March 1673, "Possessed [occupied] by Andrew Caddell, vintner." Alexander Gray's Protocol Books, I., 53, 29 Sep. 1686, "Sometime occupied by John Belches, advocate." 3. Adamson's House, No 1. Sir William Thomson's Books, II., 259, 9 July 1656, John Litill, macer. 4. Adamson's House, No. 2. Alexander Guthrie's Books, X., 137, 10 May 1600, Margaret Gray and Mr Robert Williamson. Do. do., 22 Sep. 1610, John Aitkin, Alexander Sandilands. Do. do., III., 196, 19 May 1631, the late Robert Williamson. 5. Adamson's House, No. 3. Mr Jas. Rocheid's Books, VII., 260, 18 Aug. 1684, "lately possessed [occupied] by James Clark, cook."

John Knox & Edinburgh

sometimes long after he had died. The date of the sasine of 1571 is only three months before Knox's enforced departure from Edinburgh, and no identification of the property could have been stronger than such as "presently occupied by John Knox, minister."

Mosman had property elsewhere in Edinburgh and Scotland, and the names of other tenants have been transmitted in the documents of transfer. Is there any reason for the name of the most prominent of them being omitted, except that he never was a tenant of Mosman's at all, and that if it had been known in time that the house was Mosman's, no one in the nineteenth century would ever have said he was, as no one ever said he was in the 233 years between Mosman's forfeiture and 1806? There is thus not a particle of evidence to show that Knox lived in Mosman's house before 1571, but everything points most strongly the other way. Mosman needed the house for himself, and the sasine of February 1571 shows that he took it back from his son. Mosman, besides, was a strong

"John Knox's House"

supporter of the Queen, and it was not at all natural that he should let his house to Knox, even if family necessities had not stood in the way.

But, say the supporters of the legend, whether Knox lived in Mosman's house before May 1571 or not, he lived there from August 1572 until his death in November. "It is enough for us that Knox died there"[1] There is, however, no ground for this statement. On the contrary, if Knox lived there from 1569 to 1571, his residence there again in 1572 involves the further assumption that Mosman, a notorious Romanist and zealous supporter of the Queen, hazarding and afterwards losing his life in defence of all that Knox held most abhorrent, was willing to keep his house empty for fifteen months to oblige one of his most irreconcilable foes, or turn out of his house at practically a moment's notice that the Reformer might be reinstated.

[1] "Free Church Monthly," September 1896, p. 210—"John Knox's House, Edinburgh: The property of the Free Church of Scotland." By Charles J. Guthrie, M.A., Advocate, Legal Adviser to the Free Church of Scotland.

John Knox & Edinburgh

But, again say the supporters of the legend in its most attenuated form, Mosman's house was empty, he had taken refuge with Kirkcaldy of Grange in the Castle, and he remained there until the surrender of the Castle in 1573.[1] Alas for the legend, there is again not only no proof of this statement, but there was no reason for Queen Mary's adherents to take refuge in the Castle until some weeks after the death of Knox. The historical fact is that the truce between the parties which was concluded on July 31st, 1572, for two months, was extended subsequently until the end of the year, more than a month beyond the date of Knox's death.[2] "The presumption," therefore, instead of being that Mosman "entered the Castle of Edinburgh at some date previous to Knox's death,"[3] is rather that, as a shrewd business man, he would attend to his goldsmith's booth as long as he could. Why Mosman, whose party had been in

[1] P. Hume Brown's "Life of John Knox," II., 319.
[2] P. Hume Brown's "Life of John Knox," II., 280. Hill Burton's "History of Scotland." Edit. 1897. Vol. V., p. 116.
[3] P. Hume Brown's "Life of John Knox," II., 319.

"John Knox's House"

possession of Edinburgh before the truce, should leave his house within a few days of the conclusion of the truce, in order that possibly his most dangerous foe should take undisturbed possession, is one of those mysteries of which only the necessities of an untenable position could justify the defence.

It appears thus, from the historical facts of Mosman's house, that there is not the faintest probability that Knox could ever have lived in it. This absence of any probability that Knox lived in it deepens into a certainty that Knox did not die in it, when we take into consideration the fourth and fifth points already referred to, the statements made by the authorities for what happened during Knox's last days and when on his death-bed, and the information that we have respecting the condition of his health during his residence in St Andrews in 1571-2, and the twelve weeks that was his latest period of residence in Edinburgh.

The only original authorities for Knox's final period in Edinburgh are his secretary,

John Knox & Edinburgh

Richard Bannatyne, who wrote a "Journal of the Transactions in Scotland" in the years 1570 to 1573, and Thomas Smeton's "Eximii viri Johannis Knoxii, Scoticanæ Ecclesiæ instauratoris, Vera extremæ vitæ et obitus Historia," appended to his "Responsio ad Hamiltonii Dialogum," published in Edinburgh in 1579, seven years after Knox's death. Smeton was one of Knox's intimate friends, and was appointed Principal of the University of Glasgow in 1580. Neither of these makes the slightest allusion to a house at the Netherbow, or indeed, to the locality of a house anywhere. There is nothing whatever in Bannatyne to quote relevant to the matter. He seems to have known nothing of the affecting scene so often depicted both in words and on canvas of Knox creeping down the High Street to the Netherbow, supported on the arm of a favourite attendant, with the street lined after the manner of a royal pageant with those to whom he had just been preaching in St Giles, who fell in behind their beloved pastor as he tottered feebly on.

"John Knox's House"

It will be noted in M'Crie's version that he makes no mention of the Netherbow. He adopts what are practically Smeton's words, but with amplifications, and refers to Smeton as his authority;[1] "He [Knox] descended from the pulpit, and leaning upon his staff and the arm of an attendant, crept down the street, which was lined with the audience, who, as if anxious to take the last sight of their beloved pastor, followed him until he entered his house, from which he never again came out alive." M'Crie claims the present house in a footnote as the one referred to, but Hume Brown puts it, without quoting any authority, boldly into his text, whilst omitting M'Crie's pictorial details :—" Leaning on his staff, and attended by almost the entire congregation, he made his way home to his house at the Netherbow Port."[2] Premising that Smeton himself was not an eye-witness, and that he penned his account of Knox seven years after Knox's death, we may again quote his exact words—" These things having

[1] Edition 1855, p. 270.   [2] "Life of John Knox," II., 285.

at length been performed, after he had blessed the people, with his wonted cheerful spirit, but with feeble body, and leaning on his staff, he departed to his house, accompanied by almost the whole meeting, from which he did not afterwards come forth alive." M'Crie had thus no authority for his expression "down the street," and Hume Brown has none for his "house at the Netherbow Port." We may add that the expression translated by M'Crie "audience" ("down the street, which was lined by the audience") and by Hume Brown "almost the entire congregation," may be interpreted as applying necessarily to the "elders" or "kirk-session" only.

The authorities for the period lend no countenance to the assertion that Knox went to die at the house at the Netherbow Port. The testimonies as to Knox's physical condition—the fifth point in this review of the evidence at our command—show that it was most unlikely that he would have lived at so great a distance from St Giles', and a practical im-

"John Knox's House"

possibility for him to have walked to that place after a long and fatiguing service, even though "leaning on his staff." The distance between St Giles' Church and the Netherbow is fully 410 yards. In no previous portion of the residence of Knox in Edinburgh had he lived farther than 80 yards from his church. The old manses at the west of the churchyard were still in the occupation of the former Romish clergy, and the Town Council naturally provided their minister with a manse in the immediate neighbourhood of his church, and not at the farthest corner of the burgh.

It was recognised in 1571 that Knox's years were numbered, and if he resided near St Giles' before that period, it became imperative that his house should be near it now. As early as October 1570 he "was stricken with a kind of apoplexia, called by the phisitionis resolutione, whairby the perfect vse of his tovng was stopped."[1] He wrote himself to a correspondent in May 1572 that he was "lying

[1] Bannatyne's "Transactions," Edinburgh, 1806, p. 54.

John Knox & Edinburgh

in Sanct Androis half deid"; [1] and in his will, which is dated May 13, 1572, he says—"Ane deid man haif I bene almaist thir two zeiris last bipast." Melville gives the following graphic description of his condition in these months spent in Saint Andrews as an exile from his work in Edinburgh. "I saw him everie day of his doctrine [preaching] go hulie and fear [slowly and warily], with a furring of martriks [martens] about his neck, a staff in the an hand, and guid, godlie Richard Ballenden his servant, haldin up the uther oxtar [armpit], from the Abbey to the paroche kirk, and be the said Richard and another servant lifted upe to the pulpit, whar he behovit [required] to lean at his first entrie."[2] His condition became worse after his return to Edinburgh. Killigrew, the English agent, wrote to Cecil about a month before Knox's death—"John Knox is now so feeble as scarce can he stand alone, or speak to be hard of any audience; yet doth he every Sonday cause himselfe to be

[1] Works, VI., 615, quoted in Hume Brown's "Life," II., 274.
[2] "Diary, 1556-1601," p. 26.

"John Knox's House"

carried to a place where a certayne nombre do here him, and precheth with the same vehemence and zeale that ever he did."[1] Bannatyne adds, concerning the last sermon he preached, on November 9, 1572, at the induction of Lawson as his colleague—"At that tyme [he] declared to the whole assemblie (as his waik voce wald serue, quhilk was hard but of a fewe) the dewitie of ane minister and also thair dewitie to him likwayis."[2]

After the return of Knox to Edinburgh in August 1572, he asked the Magistrates to arrange that he should preach in some smaller place than St Giles', "whare his voce might be hard, gif it were but vnto ane hundret personis."[3] They granted him the use of a room in the New Tolbooth, which had been recently built at the south-west corner of St Giles', with which it communicated through a covered way. Part of the church itself was also appropriated in connection with this build-

---

[1] Killigrew to Cecil, 6th October 1572, Knox's Works, VI., 633. Quoted in Hume Brown's "Life," II., 284.

[2] "Transactions," p. 413.

[3] Bannatyne's "Transactions," p. 286.

ing. It was here that Knox preached his last sermon, and from this that he proceeded with his audience into the body of the church to perform the ceremony of the admission of Lawson to the joint pastorate of Edinburgh.

There is thus no reason to believe that the crowd was very great which—if we are to accept Smeton's account as authentic—accompanied him afterwards to his house, even if we interpret the Latin word used by Smeton in its widest sense. But what are we to think now of the claims of a legend that makes it necessary for a man who was "half dead," and could scarcely stand alone or speak to be heard of any audience, to walk practically half the length of Edinburgh between his church and his house, even granting him the support of a staff, as put by Smeton, or the further aid of his servant's arm, in the slightly coloured reproduction of M'Crie's? It was not likely, when Knox and his friends were at liberty to return to Edinburgh, that there would be any scarcity of houses in which to shelter a dying man, and the most likely

"John Knox's House"

supposition of any is that he returned to the house he had quitted in May 1571. It has been shown that this was in all likelihood the house of John Adamson and Bessie Otterburn, for which rent is recorded to have been paid up to November 23, 1569. This house was within a few yards of the church, across the street, and a little way down a close, which would still answer to M'Crie's late embellishment of John Knox creeping down the street to his house to die. No one would ever have dreamt that he would go to Mosman's, or that Mosman's house would have been open to receive him, had it not been for the one statement made in 1806 in such an unpretending fashion, and on no authority, by the compiler of a popular guide-book to Edinburgh, that a house which would "in a few years perhaps be removed"[1] had been the residence of the "Great Scottish Reformer, John Knox."[2] (See page 161.)

The foregoing discussion has shown that

[1] "Picture of Edinburgh," by J. Stark, 1806, p. 103.
[2] Stark's "Picture," p. 103.

John Knox & Edinburgh

there was never any foundation for the statement that Knox lived at the Netherbow. It has shown further that the legend attached to the present house is an invention altogether of the present century, and that Stark, who first gave it currency in print, cannot be held responsible for its popular and varying forms. The history of the house to which the legend points has been investigated, and no room has been found for any tenancy by Knox. Lastly, it was a physical improbability, deepening into an impossibility, that Knox should have spent his last three months in life in Mosman's house. The cumulative negative evidence is overwhelming against any association of Knox the Reformer with the Netherbow.

How, then, did the legend arise? If that can be explained, it will settle all. Is there any positive evidence that would associate the name of Knox with that particular quarter of the burgh?

It so happens that there is abundant evidence in favour of what may be designated

"John Knox's House"

a positive proof that though the house at the Netherbow may have taken its modern name from a John Knox, it was not from the John Knox who died on November 24th, 1572, and was buried two days afterwards in St Giles' Churchyard.

The name of "Knox," and even of "John Knox," seems to have been a common enough one in Edinburgh during the sixteenth century. A family with that surname held property at what is now the north-east corner of the Royal Exchange for at least three generations, and a "Knox's Close" existed in this quarter in 1568. The protocol books give the names of David, Stephen, and Gilbert Knox as owners here between 1502 and 1542. The same authorities record the succession to a property in the neighbourhood of Bank Street, which had been in the possession of a William Knox before 1517, but had passed to his son and heir, John Knox, who disposed of the property in 1520.

Another "John Knox" had owned property in the quarter of the Netherbow before 1501,

John Knox & Edinburgh

and his name has been traced as descriptive of property in that neighbourhood from 1501 until 1740. This "John Knox" had been well known in his time. He was a burgess of Edinburgh, and when an identification is needed of property in a sasine it is referred to as bounded by "John Knox's" "lands" or tenements or close. So deeply had he inscribed his name on this locality that a close, formed probably on part of his property, is referred to in 1561 as "Knoxe's Close." It retains this name in 1577, 1579, 1672, 1675, and 1681. Even if it were from a later Knox that it had the name in 1561 it would strengthen the case against the Netherbow house having been the residence of the Reformer, by showing that two Knoxes had made themselves prominent in this district before that year. It appears from John Foular's protocol book that on September 17th, 1501, "Metta Knox, daughter, and one of the heirs, of the late John Knox, with the consent of John Paterson, her husband, resigned her Lands within the tenement of her said father,

"John Knox's House"

between the Land of Helen Knox, her sister, on the south, &c. &c." An entry in this same protocol book, January 17, 1501-2, in which John Knox is described as having been a burgess of Edinburgh, shows that Metta Knox possessed lands which ran from her sister's land on the High Street to the grounds of Trinity College, and that she alienated them also to the purchaser of the foregoing.

A sasine in John Stevenson's protocol book, of date December 22, 1547, describes certain property in this neighbourhood as "lying within a tenement of the late John Knox, now pertaining to Marion Crichton, Lady Rothes, on the north side of the High Street." A sasine in the protocol book of Alex. King, of date March 30, 1554, identifies another property as bounded on the east by "a tenement and Lands of the late John Knox," and another in Alex. Guthrie's protocol book, of date November 29, 1570, refers to a sale of presumably the tenement referred to on January 17, 1501-2—"a tenement of the late John Knox on the north side of the High Street."

John Knox & Edinburgh

This sasine of 1570 shows that the John Knox of the latter part of the fifteenth century was still well remembered, or that his name was considered sufficient to identify property in the neighbourhood of the Netherbow only two years before the Reformer's death. This last property is further identified in a sasine of September 3, 1577, as lying to the east of Gray's Close. Gray's Close is within 110 yards of the so-called "John Knox's House," and John Knox's property lay between the two, abutting on the north side of the High Street.

The identification of properties by reference to their relation to "the tenement of the late John Knox" continued to at least as recently as 1740.[1] A renunciation is recorded under date February 19th of that year in George Home's protocol book of an annual rent "out of a tenement of land on the north side of the High Street, on the west part of Gray's Close, between the tenement of the late John Knox, thereafter of John Rig, on the east, and the tenement of John Henderson on the west."

[1] See note page 80.

"John Knox's House"

May one not surmise that here we have tracked the legend home to its lair, and that either Stark or Stark's unknown informant had seen the name "John Knox" in some title-deeds of property in this locality, and was led immediately to the conclusion that no John Knox could be of importance but one?[1] It was a natural enough mistake and a pardonable one at the time. But a more popular use of the name Knox in the locality had, as has been already mentioned, sprung up before 1561, through its adoption as the name of a close. It appears from a comparison of the sasine of date March 30, 1554, which contains a reference to "the lands of the late John Knox," with sasines of date November 23, 1579, December 18, 1672, April 16, 1675, and March 9, 1681, that this close stood either on or immediately to the east of the lands possessed by the John Knox of 1501. The name of the close points either backward to the Knox who possessed its site sixty years

[1] This is very different from a "charge that Stark deliberately invented the tradition." See "Proceedings of S.A.Scot., 1891," pp. 346-7.

John Knox & Edinburgh

before, or to a family of that name who resided in it when the Reformer settled in Edinburgh, and who were of sufficient importance to serve as a landmark in the locality. It shows how tenacious a hold the name of Knox had taken of the neighbourhood of the Netherbow even in the days of the Reformer. Its site is marked now by Morrison's Close or by some of the buildings that extend between Morrison's Close and North Gray's Close.

The bearing of these discoveries upon the question of the residence of Knox at the Netherbow can now be stated in a few words. The study of the documents preserved in the Council Chambers shows that the name "Knox" was associated with the neighbourhood of the Netherbow for at least 240 years in the form of "the lands of the late John Knox" and "Knox's Close." But the name was never connected with Knox the Reformer until nearly 240 years after his death. We find it, then, little more than sixty years after the date of the renunciation of 1740 already quoted, again prominent in the expression

"John Knox's House"

"Knox's Land," but applied in quite another sense. The reason of the modern use of the name becomes now sufficiently explicable. A new cult of John Knox had sprung up with the advent of that evangelical spirit which gave rise afterwards to the secession known as the Free Church. The Reformer became again a popular hero, and his name and work were disentombed from the oblivion of more than two hundred years.[1] The name of Knox had during all that time hung about the Netherbow; the religious enthusiasm of the time knew of no "Knox," and especially of no "John Knox" but one; what more natural than that the designation should be seized upon as a proof

---

[1] See in confirmation of this, the admission made in M'Crie's "Life of John Knox," edition 1855, page 474,—"After slumbering for upwards of a century under a dark shade of oblivion and reproach, his character has become [since 1811] nearly as widely known and as highly admired in Scotland as it was during his lifetime, and for a century after his death." The statement that Knox's character was "widely known and . . . highly admired . . . for a century after his death" may pass in the mouth of an editor of his "Life," but requires considerable qualification so far as applies to Scotland generally and elsewhere. It acknowledges in any case that for the century and a half previous to the publication of M'Crie's "Life," that statement could not have been made.

John Knox & Edinburgh

that the old, ruined house that projected itself upon the street was the re-discovered hero's veritable home? For a time, indeed, it seemed uncertain which of the houses at the corner should gain this uncertain renown, but the opportune fall of one of them permitted the dubious "John Knox's Land" to be exchanged for the exclusive title of "John Knox's House."

"John Knox's House"

Addition to page 151.

Possibly the latest modification of the legend made in its defence is a suggestion introduced into the paper referred to on pages 127-138, which was read before the Society of Antiquaries on March 9th, 1891.[1] It is insinuated rather than stated that some of the difficulties in the way of accepting the house at the Netherbow will disappear if it is remembered that that house contains really two houses, and that "it is not at all impossible that Knox may during part of the period have only inhabited one of these houses, both of which are now included in the present John Knox's house." The whole force of the argument in the two pages from which this quotation is taken is to show that Knox may have been living in Mosman's house in 1563, and by implication that he may have lived there from 1563 to 1572. It was ren-

---

[1] "Proceedings of S.A.Scot., 1891," p. 345: "Is John Knox's House entitled to the name?" by Charles J. Guthrie, advocate, F.S.A.Scot.

dered necessary by the discovery that Knox was living then in a "back-land," that is, in a house which did not front the High Street.[1]

This suggestion that Knox only inhabited part of the house is one that is likely to commend itself to any subsequent defenders of the authenticity of the Netherbow house, and deserves on that account at least a passing notice. Apart from the fact that it has been proved from official documents that Knox lived in Mowbray's house in the present Warriston's Close in 1563, there is no reason for the suggestion that Mosman's house was at that period anything but "in all probability one large house in occupation of the builder and owner" (MacGibbon and Ross's "Castellated and Domestic Architecture of Scotland," IV., 424). It is, therefore, satisfactory to find that the author of the suggestion has withdrawn it, also by implication, in his recent handbook to the present Netherbow house, "written . . . at the request of the

[1] See Mowbray's Sasine to Scot. 1565, March 28, "The Backlands of the said Robert Mowbray;" also the sasines of September 23, 1568, and May 1st, 1629.

"John Knox's House"

General Trustees of the Free Church of Scotland, to whom John Knox's house belongs." "When the whole house was occupied by one household, access to the upper storeys from the street was got through the rooms in the first floor; but when the upper storeys were tenanted by a separate family, it became necessary to provide direct access to them from the street. This forestair, to use the old expression, although not belonging to the original structure, is now one of the few survivals of those outside stairs which were a characteristic feature of old Edinburgh houses."[1] As a matter of fact, Mosman's house was divided into two houses or more by the beginning of the seventeenth century, but it is safe to abide by the evidence furnished by the construction of the house itself, that it was originally built for a single dwelling. This same writer, indeed, adopts that view in another part of the same paper, when it was necessary to show that the house was

[1] "John Knox and John Knox's House," by Charles John Guthrie, Q.C., F.S.A.Scot., 1898, p. 27.

worthy of Knox,—"the amount and character of the rest of the house accord with the amount and character of the accommodation which a man in Knox's position might be expected to possess."[1]

The sentence preceding this, which is indicated by the word "rest," reads as follows: —"Inside the house (Mosman's house) a room is now shown as John Knox's study, which has not only a traditional right to that name, but exactly accords with that 'warm study of daills' (that is, as I take it, lined with deals) which the Town Council ordered to be made for John Knox in 1561." It has been shown that Knox could not have lived in Mosman's house in 1561, and that this "study of daills" was built in Mowbray's house in the close now called "Warriston's Close;" but the insistence on the size of Mosman's house affording a presumption that it is "Knox's house" permits the adduction of another proof, if additional proof were required, that it could not have

[1] "Proceedings of S.A.Scot., 1891," p. 336.

"John Knox's House"

been his residence in 1561, and that the new study was not erected there. The house in which the study was built must have been a comparatively small one and not above two storeys in height. The Dean of Guild's accounts for the year 1561 contain an item of eight shillings for stripping the slates off the roof of the house to permit a window being put in the "said studie."[1] The so-called "study" in the present house is on the second floor,[2] and not near the roof, which is, and always was, two storeys higher up, so that there could have been no reason for breaking the roof so as to allow a window to be inserted. It is agreed on all hands that Mosman's house was built originally to about its present height, but a copy of the contract still exists which shows that considerable alterations were made on Mowbray's

---

[1] "At the tirwinge (stripping) of ane pairt of the sklattis of the said ludgeinge for brokin of ane wyndo to the said studie, to ane pure man for taking furth of the reid (rubbish) . . . viij^{s.}"

[2] "Above, on the second floor, are the three rooms specially associated by tradition with Knox's residence, . . . the little room in the wooden casing of the house, his study." "John Knox and John Knox's house," by C. J. Guthrie, p. 28.

house in 1614, when permission was obtained from the opposite proprietor to raise the wall which faced his property, and construct an outside stair to the height of two feet above the original level of this wall, with a view, no doubt, of affording an access to the apartments which would be formed above the original roof.[1]

[1] Burgh Register of Deeds, vol. 15, 18th July 1614. There was, of course, no obligation to obtain the permission of the proprietor opposite for the construction of the new rooms. Permission was necessary only in so far as there was danger of encroachment on his rights.

"John Knox's House"

STARK'S ACCOUNT OF JOHN KNOX'S HOUSE.

The following is the full text of Stark's reference to "John Knox's House," on which so circumstantial a legend was founded:—

"Among the antiquities of Edinburgh may be mentioned the house of the great Scottish Reformer, John Knox. It stands on the north side of the foot of the High Street, and, projecting into the street, reduces it nearly one half of its width. On the front to the west is a figure in *alto relievo*, pointing up with its finger to a radiated stone, on which is sculptured the name of the Divinity in three different languages:

ΘΕΟΣ
DEUS
GOD

Whether the figure is meant to represent the reformer himself, or not, is not known; but whoever it is, he seems to have been hardly used, part of the stone on which it is

John Knox & Edinburgh

executed being broken off either by accident or design. The edifice itself is one of the oldest stone houses in Edinburgh. As in the course of the improvements of the city, this building will, in a few years perhaps be removed, it is to be wished that the sculptured stones could be preserved, in memory of a man who, whatever were his faults, by his bold eloquence, and undaunted conduct, pulled down the fabric of a superstition which had shackled the mind for ages.—"Picture of Edinburgh," 1806, pages 102, 103.

M'Crie's only reference to the house is given in the text, page 121. The differences between these original statements, if even they can be called original, and the subsequent embellished and circumstantial forms of the legend, are obvious.

Index

Abercrombie, Alexander, vintner, 83.
Accounts of the Treasurer of Edinburgh, 15.
Adamson, Alexander, 92, 93, 98, 103.
—— James, payment to him on account of John Knox, 33; appointed to procure contributions from the faithful, 36, 104.
—— John, his house occupied by John Knox, 48, 49; tenements belonging to him, 88-112; was with Knox at St Andrews, 107; his house, 139 n.
—— Robert, 70, 71.
Adamson's Close, 97, 98.
Aitken, John, merchant, 95, 96; 139 n.
—— Robert, 95, 96.
Ancrum Moor, battle of, 4.
Arbukill, John, 70, 71.
Argyll, Earl of, 19.
Arran, the Earl of, 14.
Arres, John, 136.
—— Mariot, 137.

Bad, John, armourer, 17.
Bailie Brown's Close, 98 n.
Bailie, Robert, merchant, Edinburgh, 100 n.
Baird, Sir Robert, of Saughton Hall, 110.
Balfour, Gilbert, master of the town's artillery, 12.
Balleny, Thomas, 100 n.
Balmerino, Lord, his house, 117.
Bank of Scotland, 69, 91, 97.
Bank Street, 153.
Bannatyne, Richard, secretary to John Knox, 144, 148, 149.
Barron, James, treasurer, 31, 32, 36.
Baxter, James, wright, 22.
Belsches, John, advocate, 111, 139 n.
Beaton, Cardinal, assassinated, 6, 76.
Beyr, Sir John, chaplain, 27.
Bonkill, Alexander, 91.
—— Marion, 103.
Borthwick, Alexander, vintner, 99.
Bothwell, Adam, Bishop of Orkney, 108.
—— Earl of, 8, 39, 108.
Bowes, Marjorie, wife of John Knox, 75.
Bradie, Mungo, goldsmith, 47.
Brown, John, his property identified with the site of Mowbray's house, 76-81, 85, 86.
—— younger, executed for heresy, 76, 85.
—— Murdoch, tenant, 139 n.
—— P. Hume, his "Life of John Knox," 129, 142 n, 145, 146, 149 n.
—— Robert, bookseller, 99.
—— Thomas, bookseller, 95 n.
Bruce of Binning, 82 n, 109.

Index

Bruce of Stonehouse and Airth, 109.
Bruce's Close, 82, 83, 84, 109.
Bruntisland, artillery of, visited, 16.
Buccleuch statue, the, 106.
Buchanan, Thomas, Master of the High School, 60.
Bull's Close, 100, 101.
Byer's Close, 109.

Caddell, Andrew, vintner 139 n.
Caichepeele Close, 101, 104.
Cairns, John, reader in St Giles' Church, 32-35, 40, 44, 45, 53, 56, 65-67.
Calderwood ——, wife of Thomas Brown, 95 n.
Caldour, Robert, gunner, 12.
Canongate, the, 56.
Cant, Jonet, 78.
Carberry Hill, 39.
Carkettill, Elizabeth, 76, 77, 80.
Ceraris, John, 93.
Chalmers, John, servant to Knox, 59.
Chambers, Robert, author of "Traditions of Edinburgh," 122, 123, 124.
Charles I., King, 94 n, 110.
Charters, Henry, 82.
—— Thomas, merchant, 82.
Charterhouse, the, 28.
Chatelherault, Duke of, 75, 111.
Chester, in England, 59 n.
Cheviots, the, 4.
Chisholm, Thomas, 77, 80.
Clark, James, cook, 139 n.
Clerihugh's tavern, 111, 112.
Clerk, Alexander, collector for the ministers' stipends, 37.
Cockburn Street, 85, 104.
—— Hotel, 87.
Coke, Thomas, artilleryman, 16.
"Congregation," the Lords of the, 8, 14, 15, 19, 30.

Corporation of Edinburgh, owners of the site of John Knox's House, 79, 87.
Corstorphine, collegiate church of, 68.
Council Chamber and Burgh Court (the new) cover the site of Knox's House, 87, 88.
Cowgate, the, 22, 68.
Craig, Mr John, minister, 28, 39, 40; furnishing of his house, 56; his travelling expenses paid, 58; takes the ministry in St Giles', in Knox's absence, 61.
Craig, Sir Lewis, 110.
—— Sir Thomas, 110.
Craig's Close, 109.
Craigcrook, the prebendary of, 27.
Crawfurd, James, priest, 27.
Crichton, Marion, Lady Rothes, 155.
Crighton, Patrick, of Lugton, 90, 91, 93, 97.
Cromwell's residence in Edinburgh, 69.
Cunyngham, John, 91.

Darnley murdered, 10, 39; offended at Knox's preaching, 60.
Dean of Guild's Accounts, references to payments on account of John Knox, therein, 49-53; to the ministers, 59; accounts, 65, 164.
Dean of Guild Court, proceedings anent Knox's Land, 117, 118.
Dieppe, 10.
Dryburgh Abbey, 5.
Dryden, Mr, tenant at Netherbow, 122.
Duf, David, armourer, 17.
Dunbar, ammunition sent to, 17.

Index

Dunbar, battle of, 69.
Dunbar's Close, 69, 72.
Dundee, visit of Knox to, 10.
Dunfermline, the Abbot of, 45, 72.
Durie, John, tailor, 45, 72, 74.

Edinburgh, burnt, 4, 6; age of its buildings, 5; riot in, 7; state of, 14, 15, etc.
—— Castle of, 5, 9, 142.
—— Cross of, 9; Market Cross, 111.
—— the Fleshmarket, 19; Mid Fleshmarket Close, 99, 101.
—— the Flesh House, 20.
—— the High Street, 20, 68, 70, 71, 76, 92, 105, etc.
—— Greyfriars' Port, 20, 21.
—— High School, 60.
—— Netherbow, 16, 17, 20; Knox's supposed House at, 115-121, etc.
—— the Overbow, 28.
—— Tolbooth of, 29, 68.
—— the Town Council of, their preparations against invasion, 11, 12; accept the Reformation, 15, 22; their care for the spiritual wants of the citizens, 25, 29-40; their liberality to the Reformed Ministers, 56-61; choose representative elders to the General Assembly, 59, etc.
Elizabeth, Queen of England, 8, 68.
English, the, policy of, towards Scotland, 5-7, 13, 30.
Erskine, Lord, 14.
Eymouth (Haymouth), ammunition sent to, 17.

Fairlie (Fernlie), David, 78, 79, 81.
Finlay (Fynlaw), Robert, 94 n.

Forbes, Patrick, merchant, 94.
Forrester, Adam, Provost of Edinburgh, 68.
Forresters of Corstorphine, 68.
Forrester's Wynd, 68, 69, 97.
Forrester, David (Forster), collector for the ministers, 35, 44, 65; his house, 66-68, 108.
Forth, the Firth of, 4.
Foulis, Mr James, of Colinton, 76.
—— Mr Robert, advocate, 82.
Fountain Well, the, 121.
France, the Scots' alliance with, 5; a force from, sent against St Andrews, 6.
Frier, Matthew, baker, 117.

Gavinlock, Alexander, mason, 96.
Gavinlock's Land, 97.
Geneva, 8; Knox retires to, 9; Goodman his Colleague there, 59 n.
Gilbert, Michael, gunner, 16.
Glasgow, the Archbishop of, 111.
Glencairn, Earl of, 19.
Goodman, Christopher, minister of St Andrews, 58, 59.
Gourlay, George, officer, 40.
Gray, Alexander, notary, 139 n.
—— Margaret, 139 n.
—— Robert, gets payments for damages to his herbs and flowers, 15.
Gray's Close, 156, 158.
Green, William, & Sons, publishers, 91.
Guthrie, Alexander, Dean of Guild, 57.
—— Alexander, Town Clerk of Edinburgh, 77, 139 n, 155.
—— C. J., advocate, his papers on John Knox's house, 116 n, 127, 128, 134, 135, 138 n, 141 n, 160, 164.

Index

Haltoun, the Laird of, 91, 103.
Hannay, Mr James, Dean of St Giles', 94 *n*.
Henderson, John, 156.
Henrison, Thomas, treasurer, 49.
Hepburn, Margaret, 66, 70, 89.
Hepburne, Robert, of Whitburgh, 99.
Heriot, Franciscetta, 93, 94.
Heriot, George, elder, goldsmith, 92, 93.
—— George, younger, 92.
—— Patrick, 93.
Heriot's Close, 98 *n*.
Heriot's Hospital, Governors of, 94.
Hertford, the Earl of, 4, 137.
Holyrood Abbey, 5.
Home, George, notary, 156.
Hope, Charles, of Hopetoun, 83.
—— Edward, appointed to procure support for the ministers, 36.
—— Sir James of Hopetoun, 82.
Hopper, Janet, 76.
—— Katherine, 76, 77.
—— Mr Richard, 81.
—— Robert, 78, 79.
Huguenots in France massacred, 9.
Hunter, Mungo, smith, 22.
Hunter's Square, 92, 104, 105.
Huntly, the Earl of, 14.

Inglis, John, mason, 21.
Ireland, David, 70.
—— John, 69, 70.
—— Patrick, 66; his house, 70-73, 89, 108.
Ireland's Close, 69, 72.

Jackson, John, 82.
James III., King, 109.
James VI., King, 110.
Jedburgh Abbey, 5.

Johnston, Sir Archibald of Warriston, 110, 111.
—— John, writer, 46.

Kar, Robert, appointed to collect for the ministers' stipend, 37.
Kelle, William, gunner, 12.
Kelso Abbey, 5.
Kerr, Andrew, 96 *n*.
Killigrew, the English Ambassador, 68, 149 *n*.
King, Alexander, town clerk, 89.
—— Janet, wife of James Mosman, 138.
Kirkcaldy, Sir William, of Grange, holds the Castle of Edinburgh, 10, 11, 107, 142.
Kirk of Field Port, 21.
Knox, David, Gilbert, and Stephen, owners of property near the Royal Exchange, 153.
—— Helen, 155.
—— John, in 1520, sells property near Bank Street, 153.
—— John, owner of property at Nether Bow, 153-158.
—— Metta, 154, 155.
Knox's Close, 153, 154, 158.
Knox's House, the Legend of, 115, *et seq*.
KNOX, JOHN, minister, his place of residence in Edinburgh, v, vi; a captive in France, and life in England, 9; his effigy burnt, *ibid.*; at Dieppe, 10; his movements in Scotland, *ibid.*; minister of Edinburgh, 11, 29; records of his connection with the city, 30-34; his house furnished, 31, 32; payment of stipend to him, 32, 33; his house-rent paid, 42-44; proposed change of residence, 45; lodged in

Index

Mowbray's house, 46; in John Adamson's house, 48, 49; at St Andrews, 49; in Angus and Mearns, 57, 58; goes to the Assembly at Perth, 60; prohibited from preaching, 60; houses occupied by him in Edinburgh, 65-112; his first settled residence, 73; a warm study ordered for him, 75, 86-88; at St Andrews, 107; his will referred to, 107, the Legend of the Netherbow House, 115-168; "John Knox's Land," 117-120, 159, 160.

Knox, William, owner of property near Bank Street, 153.

Knoxes, a family of, located near the Netherbow since the 15th century, 153.

Langside, battle of, 8, 39.
Lauder, Gilbert, 93.
Lawson, Mr James, colleague to John Knox, 121, 149.
Leis, Andrew, blackfriar, 29.
Leith, the French land at, 6; houses repaired at, 21.
Lesley, south parks of, 100 *n*.
Lessels, Alexander, merchant, 95 *n*.
—— John, merchant, burgess of Haddington, 95 *n*.
Lithgow, Sir John, 27.
Litill, John, macer, 139 *n*.
Litstair, James, armourer, 17.
Loughborough, rectory of, 55.
Lowrie, Margaret, wife of James Riddell, 96 *n*.
Lowrye, James, collector for the stipends, 37.
Lundy, David, 77.

MacLeod, Æneas, 84.
Maisson, Margaret, wife of Robert Finlay, 94 *n*.

Maistertoun, James, 139 *n*.
Mary King's Close, 84, 85, 86.
Mary, Queen of Scots, state of affairs after her arrival, 35, 36, *notes*; prohibits Knox from preaching, 60; her marriage with Bothwell, 108, 137, 142.
Mary of Lorraine, the Queen Dowager, 14, 15; Regent, 18; her death, 54.
Maxton, John, 91, 99,
M'Calzeane, James, 70.
M'Calyeane Mr Thomas, 12, 71; of Cliftonhall, advocate, 82 *n*, 93, 108.
M'Crie, Dr, his Life of Knox, 120, 123, 124, 125, 126, 133, 145, 146, 150, 151, 159, 167.
Mein, John, 139 *n*.
Melrose Abbey, 5.
Merse, the, Knox's visit to, 59.
Miller, Mr Peter, his papers on Knox's house, 126, 127.
Milne, Robert, of Balfarg, King's master mason, 83-87.
Morison, John, gunner, 17.
Morrison's Close, 158.
Morton, the Earl of, 68.
Mosman, James, owner of house at the Netherbow, 129, 134 *n*, 136, 137, 139 *n*, 140-143, 151, 152, 161-165.
—— John, goldsmith, 137.
Mowbray, Andrew, 43, 77, 78.
Mowbray, Robert, his house tenanted by John Knox, vi, 43, 45, 46, 73, 74, 77-79, 106, 161 *n*.
Murray, James, of Philiphaugh, Lord of Session, 111.

Napier, Helen, 77.
Netherbow, the (see Edinburgh), the house there popularly known as "John Knox's House," 115-168.

Index

Newbottill, convent of, 91, 102.
Newlands, Robert, glover, 98-100.
—— Robert, younger, 98, 99.
Newlands' Land, 100, 102.
Newton, Elizabeth, wife of Patrick Forbes, 94.
Nichole, James, collector for the stipends, 37.
Nithsdale, visit of Knox to, 59.
North Loch, the, 7, 16, 21, 70, 71, 76-78, 80, 93, 103.

Otterburne, Bessie, wife of John Adamson, 48, 88-90, 95, 98, 103, 151.

Park, Alexander, treasurer, 44, 45, 59, 65, 72.
Perth, visited by Knox, 10, monasteries of, attacked, 18; General Assembly at, 60.
Pinkie, battle of, 5.
Pleydell, Counsellor, 112.
Poultry Market, the, 92, 101.
Preston, Mr John, collector for the ministers, 35, 36.
Purves, John, deacon of the tailors, 37.

Rae, Hector, merchant, 92.
Randolph, the English Ambassador, 75.
Reformation in Scotland, 5, 8, 9, 10, 22, 39.
—— in England, 8.
—— in France, 8.
Reid, William, merchant, 100 n.
Riddell, James, 96 n.
Rigg, Hugh, 77.
—— John, 156.
Rizzio, David, slain, 10.
Robin Hood, games suppressed, 35 n.
Rocheid, Mr James, notary, 139 n.
Roman clergy, the, provided for at the Reformation, 25, 26, 29.
Royal Exchange Buildings, 85, 153.
Salt Tron, the, 99, 101, 103-105.
Sandilands, Alexander, 139 n.
Schange, Patrick, joiner, 50.
Scotland, condition of, before the Reformation, 3-8.
Scotsman, the, proprietors of, 104.
Scott, Mr John, of Tarvet, 81.
—— Robert, writer, 43, 44; his wife craves for rent due for Knox's lodging, 47; seized in Mowbray's property, 79.
—— Thomas, clerk to the Signet, 100 n.
—— Sir Walter, 112.
Seton, Lord, Provost of Edinburgh, 12, 67, 108.
Sklater, Andrew, Bailie, 78.
Smeton, Mr Thomas, author of an account of Knox, 121, 144, 150.
Smith, Mrs Robert, 139 n.
Smyth, Andrew, 139 n.
Speir, Rachel, 81.
—— Sarah, 82.
—— Thomas, merchant, 81, 82.
Spens, John, 58.
St Andrews, Bishop of, appeal from, by the Council of Edinburgh, 16.
—— Christopher Goodman, minister of, 58.
—— John Knox at, 49, 107, 143.
—— Castle of, 6, 9.
Standsfield, Sir James, of Newmilns, 102.
Stark, J., author of the "Picture of Edinburgh," 116, etc., 133, 152, 157, 166.

Index

St Bartholomew, massacre of Protestants on his festival, 9.
Steill, Patrick, merchant, 83-87.
Stevenson, John, notary, 155.
Stevinson, Andrew, treasurer, 48.
Stewart, Adam, 76.
—— Helen, 76, 77.
—— Sir James, of Kirkfield, Knight, Provost of Edinburgh, 95 *n*.
—— John, writer, 100 *n*.
—— Margaret, second wife of John Knox, 75, 111.
St George's Church, 125.
St Giles' Church, 5; image of the saint burned, 7; law plea thereon, 16; ornaments taken to the castle, 13; jewels and stalls secured, 17, 18; "purged of idolatry," 19; the steeple fortified, 20; chaplains appointed, 26; St James's altar, 28; the churchyard of, 29; thanksgiving in the church, 30; Willock's ministry therein, 54; John Craig's ministry, 61; the churchyard, 105; Knox's last sermon in, 121, 144, 146, 147, 149; Knox buried in the churchyard, 153.
St Giles Street, 69, 91, 97, 105.
Strachan, Alexander, notary, 139 *n*.
Surrey, Earl of, invades Scotland, 6.
Sym, Mr Alexander, advocate, 16.
Symson, John, 90.

Tennand, Francis, his tenement, 90.
Tennand, Mungo, 90.
Teviotdale, Knox to visit, 59.
Thomson, Mr Alexander, minister, 94.
—— Margaret, wife of Alexander Lessels, 95.
—— Sir William, notary, 139 *n*.
Tod, George, gunner, 20.
Tolbooth, the old, 93, 96, 97.
—— the new, Knox preaches therein, 149.
Trinity College, Hospital of, 29; grounds of, 155.
Tron, the Salt, 99, 101, 103-105.
Tron Church, the, 104, 112 *n*.

Urquhart, Sir George, of Cromarty, 110.

Warriston's Close, 82 *n*, 84-87, 109, 111, 161, 165.
Watson, Robert, 55, 83.
Williamson, Robert, 139 *n*.
Willok, John, preacher, 53-55, 59, 67.
Wilson, Sir Daniel, his "Memorials of Edinburgh," 117, 122, 126-129.
—— William, of Soonhope, 100 *n*.
Wishart, George, burning of, 6.
Wrightslands, Lord, 110.
Writers to the Signet, Society of, 85.
Writers' Court, 85, 111.

Young, Thomas, of Rosebank, 84.
—— Walter, 70, 71.

www.ingramcontent.com/pod-product-compliance
Lightning Source LLC
Chambersburg PA
CBHW072133160426
43197CB00012B/2086